Flying without Fear

The author learned to fly in 1961. In 1964 he was the youngest pilot in the UK to hold a flying instructor's rating. In 1965 he was the chief flying instructor of the largest flying club in the country. During his twenty-eight year career with a major British airline his training skills were recognised for their innovation, effectiveness and popularity. Now retired from commercial flying he is a CAA examiner in Human Factors.

FLYING WITHOUT FEAR

Captain Keith Godfrey

MacroTeach publications

First published in 2003 by Macroteach Publications
Old School House, Shell Lane, Colemore, Nr Alton
Hampshire GU34 3RX
Reprinted 2005, 2007

Distributed by Littlehampton Book Services Ltd
Faraday Close, Durrington, Worthing, BN13 3RB
Tel 01903 828511, Fax 01903 8288801/802, e-mail orders@lbsltd.co.uk

Illustrations by Gordon Redrup

British Library Cataloguing in Publication Data
A catalogue record for this book is available from the British Library

ISBN 0-9542828-0-9

Typeset by Amolibros, Milverton, Somerset
Printed and bound by T J International Ltd, Padstow, Cornwall, UK

CONTENTS

Visit flying withoutfear.com for

Over 100 pages of Free help including

Free help forum

Assessments

Hints and tips

Audio files

Podcasts

Quizzes

Videos

Blog

flyingwithoutfear.com is the biggest fear of flying resource in the world

INTRODUCTION

My interest in writing this book is entirely selfish. I hope that someone else will be encouraged to write a book about the fear of being at sea.

Flying, despite what you may feel inside, is safe by every measurable standard. You've got more chance of winning the lottery than being involved in an air incident. And if you are involved in an incident you've got more chance of surviving than not winning the lottery. Statistically you'd have to fly every day for 19,000 years to be involved in a serious incident. The chances of being injured are even less.

I've flown over 20,000 hours. I have never been involved in a serious incident and never had an engine stop in flight. I've been struck by lightning twelve times. I have only once had to divert to another airport because of poor weather. I have never been involved in a near miss or any hazardous situation involving Air Traffic Control. I have never had to divert because of a shortage of fuel and I've done countless automatic landings.

And when people ask me what was the most dangerous thing that ever happened to me in my flying career I say, 'I met a girl in a bar in the Far East who turned out to be a man.'

And I had to make that up because nothing exciting ever happened to me.

———

Before I answer your questions here are some thoughts about flying in general and about being a passenger.

➢ What is normal, and safe, to me as an experienced airline captain is probably not what you would call normal, and you should try to bear this in mind when you are flying. And because it's not normal to you, that doesn't mean it's dangerous.

> A modern aircraft can withstand enormous forces. It can fly with the nose pointing way up or way down, it can bank as steeply as any other aircraft, it is able to fly at a speed much higher than its normal maximum speed, and it can fly much more slowly than it ever does when you are on board.

> It is capable of carrying more weight than it does on a commercial flight even when flying full of passengers, full of fuel and filled with cargo.

> It can stop on the runway in a shorter distance than you will ever experience. Pilots never use the brakes to their maximum effect. It can land harder than you will ever experience and will not need repairing or maintenance. It can fly in turbulence so violent that the wings will distort. But none of these things will damage an aircraft.

> The modern airliner flies within a very narrow band of its real capabilities. When it is designed the engineers build more safety features into it than it really needs, or will ever use. It's the 'just-in-case factor'. It's built stronger than it needs to be and all sorts of devices alert pilots when they are getting near the limits of what they are allowed to do. And that's not what the aircraft can do, it's what they, the pilots, are allowed to do.

> Test pilots check all these safety features and fly an aircraft way beyond the limits to make sure that the safety margins are big enough.

> Before an aircraft is introduced into service the airlines themselves make it even safer by restricting the things that pilots are allowed to do, such as not climbing as steeply as the plane is capable of doing. The airlines will insist on ultra-

The modern airliner flies within a very narrow band of its real capabilities.

safe practices. A typical example is that the wheels are put down about four minutes before landing even though they only take twenty seconds to go down.

➤ The laws that govern the operation of aircraft, throughout the world include rules such as requiring that the pilots not only have to check things individually but must confirm with each other that checks are done. Pilots are required to work as a team.

> It is beyond dispute that Air Transport is the most regulated and safety directed industry of any, and aviation leads the way in safety and training: check after check, safety measure after safety measure.

> The aircraft you fly in is capable of doing so much but is allowed to do so little. The pilots' skills are rarely used to a maximum. The whole industry operates in an environment of safety measures.

If you can, while you are flying, try to separate what you can see is going on from what you can feel. Your feelings are likely to mislead you. Pilots don't rely on their sensations when they're flying the aircraft, they have to look at their instrument indications; there is no other way to know what position the aircraft is in. Our balancing system is dependent upon our eyes being able to see the horizon, or something to tell us which way is up.

In the cabin you don't have a set of instruments to confirm what's going on. You only have your thoughts and sensations to go by. As a passenger you can only imagine what the aircraft is doing, and you know from fairground rides that what you feel is different from what you see. When different sources of information to our brains conflict we find it hard to make sense of them so we become uneasy and feel threatened. We interpret this as danger.

When we 'fly' nervous passengers in our flight simulator, during our nervous flyers' course, we spend the first part of the flight without any simulator movement at all, and it's quite amazing how people re-evaluate their perceptions.

For the first time they can see what is happening without the feeling of being thrown around. Having seen that, the next part of the flight is done with 'movement' on, as we say, and our passengers can concentrate on the sounds, noises and actual movements without being distracted by emotions and sensations.

About those 'noises'

Any sudden noise should startle us, it's the way we've evolved over millions of years. When we hear a noise we take 'flight' mentally or physically while we decide whether the noise is friendly or not. It's a defence mechanism that keeps us safe from unfamiliar events. It's called our startle response.

On an aircraft there are all sorts of sudden noises. Noises that we can't interpret because generally, we've had little or no previous experience of them. But nature still sends a shot of adrenaline through our bodies to prepare us for 'fight or flight'. Normally we would retreat to somewhere safe, work out what's happening and then return. But we can't change our hiding place on an aircraft. We just have to sit there. We're stuck in a hostile environment where we can't do the thing that aeons of evolution urge us to do. So we do the next thing we're programmed for, and that is we worry. Worry and uncertainty make us fear the worst.

Worry varies from mild nervousness to outright panic. And it gets worse with time because those feelings of fear go into our long-term memory programme and wait, ready to take charge of our feelings at the next reminder. So we are constantly re-enforcing our fears without realising that we are doing so. And our feelings of fear during the wait are often worse than the reality we're preparing for.

So, when you're flying and you hear or see something that you don't understand, just ask a member of cabin crew to explain. Or ask the passenger sitting next to you. Don't just sit there being brave.

The noises from the speedbrakes (things that come up on the top of the wings to slow the aircraft down), the noise from the undercarriage and the flaps cause aerodynamic noise (explained later) and they all cause buffeting of the aircraft, which makes the aircraft shake. The faster an aircraft is flying, the greater the noise and buffeting will be when the wheels, flaps or speedbrakes are used. The engines make a lot of noise too, and different aircraft engines make different noises. The more engine power that is used the more noise the engines will make. When the speedbrakes, wheels or flaps are used, more power is needed to overcome the resistance to the airflow. So the chances are you won't get one noise, you'll get several.

When the wheels and flaps and speedbrake are being used, the aircraft is probably preparing for landing so there will be lots of movement of the aircraft. The same applies after take-off, of course. So when you're getting the noise you're getting the shaking, while you get the shaking you're getting the sensations of movement.

I'm surprised any of us fly.

Start here, though:

➢ Say to yourself…the noise is because of the speedbrakes, flaps, wheels or engines.
➢ Remind yourself…when speedbrakes, flaps, wheels are used more power is needed.
➢ Remember that…when more power is needed there's more noise from the engines.
➢ Compliment yourself when you recognise that the buffeting is caused by the different airflow when speedbrakes, flaps, wheels are used, because you are making progress towards overcoming your fears.

When you get an opportunity, take a casual look around the cabin and find the most nervous-looking passengers, because it's likely that they'll be pilots positioning for another flight. Even though they understand all the noises, procedures and sensations, they often look nervous. Why should they, of all people, be nervous? Is it because they have reason not to trust the pilots?

No, it's much more obvious than that. They are back-seat drivers, they want to be in control.

Control is what society claims to give us now. We can control when we work, buy our food, when we get money from the bank, go to the cinema and do countless other things. We don't have to rely on many other people to organise our lives. And when we do have to hand over control on trains, buses and cars we believe that we have enough knowledge of the risks to choose whether to accept them or not.

Why is it though, that many of us happily hand control to a doctor or a dentist? (OK, maybe I'm wrong to associate dentist and happy for anyone over thirty years of age.) I think we are willing to hand control to someone else because we believe that things are going to improve, that's the implied agreement.

We may not fully understand all the details but we feel the trade-off is worth it. In the dentist's or doctor's surgery, more pain now may be worth it, for less pain later.

But as soon as you think about flying you realise that you are handing control of your life over to someone else—the pilots: two pilots that you don't know, can't see, and don't trust entirely.

But in reality you're giving control to people better trained than doctors or dentists, and who are checked for competency every two months. Doctors do not have checks on their competence as formally and frequently as pilots or aircraft engineers.

For instance, less than a week before I retired I had to do an eight-hour competency check in the simulator to maintain my licence, even though I was on leave.

What was I likely to get wrong during a week's leave that I hadn't got wrong in thirty-five years? There are no exceptions in aviation for anyone, at any time.

And don't worry that the pilot may be short of vital information. Pilots are given enormous amounts of pre-flight information about the aircraft, the airfields, the airways, taxiways, runways, and the weather. There is no time during a flight when a pilot has to wonder about information; everything is made available to him. And he is required by law to check it, before flight and during flight, then make reports after the flight.

But I know that reassurance is not the thing that really matters when you're nervous so we'll get on with 'your' part of the book.

Here are some of the questions I was asked during my career as a pilot. And some that people asked me when they found out I was writing this book.

I hope that reading it makes flying a bit easier for you.

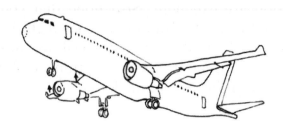

HELLO EVERYONE,

I'm Keith Godfrey the Captain, welcome aboard this flight 'Bookworm Zero One'.

I hope that you're all making yourselves comfortable. We're just completing our preparations here on the flight deck and we shall be leaving in just a few moments. May I please draw your attention to, and may I stress the importance of listening to, the cabin crew safety briefing which they will be giving after we have started the engines. Our flight time is two hours and twenty minutes and we shall be cruising at a height of 35,000 feet. Weather conditions en route are good and the landing conditions at our destination are excellent. So I hope that you'll be able to sit back, relax and enjoy your flight with us today. Later in the flight I shall speak to you again but in the meantime if there is anything at all that I can do for you, please let me know.

Chapter One

SIMPLE THINGS THAT I'VE ALWAYS WANTED TO ASK

How long could you stay up if the engines stopped at 35,000 feet?

If the engines stopped at cruising height you can glide for 30 minutes before you're on the ground. You could glide about 120 miles. All the controls work as if the engines were still going.

What are the things that make passengers most nervous?

Noises most of all, unexpected movements of the aircraft, not being in control of what's going on, not understanding what's going on and turbulence.

What can be done about it?

Read a book like this and get some information. Perhaps go to a 'talk-in' for nervous passengers. Have a flight simulator experience. Attend a nervous flyers' course. Or go on a nervous flyers' flight. There are also phone lines where you can talk to pilots.

Which is the best?

The one that addresses your needs.

How do they work?

They work because the courses give you the chance to ask the questions that bother you. And the more expensive ones can give you an actual flight experience under closely controlled conditions. But my suggestion is that you choose a course where the flight experience is optional. If you are nervous of flying you may not want to take the flight at the end of the course. This would be a perfectly natural feeling. Do not see that choice as failure.

Do a course and then, when you're ready, take a flight later with the course providers.

Do most people worry about the same things?

Yes, there are certain things that most people are nervous about: turbulence, noise, movement, loss of control and sensations.

Some people fly for years and are still nervous: does that mean that these fears are very hard to overcome?

No, it just means that even in years and years of flying you don't get very much experience of actually being in the air. And the bad feelings that we have always find re-enforcement.

Why do things often seem to get worse rather than better?

'Seem to' are the right words to describe this. There is evidence that stress builds up over a period of time. Although people subjected to constant stress find coping strategies, they still experience stress. People who are nervous of flying are always building up a bank of bad feelings in exactly the same way that we build up good feelings about things we like. From my experience of nervous flyers, it doesn't take much to turn bad feelings into good ones. Knowledge, help and confidence are key ingredients.

Is it true that some people are happy to fly, then suddenly, on one flight, things are so terrifying that they become frightened forever?

It appears so but it's not really the case. What happens is that people hear stories of dreadful flights then expect the same thing to happen to them. In the meantime they become more and more nervous, more and more apprehensive until they talk themselves, and everyone else, into one bit of turbulence being 'the worst flight ever'.

That's the magic word isn't it...turbulence?

Yes, it certainly seems to be. It's the word that always used to come up when passengers visited me on the flight deck.

So what is turbulence?

Turbulence is the irregular movement of the air. When air travels across the ground it hits things like buildings, towns, hills and mountains and causes the air to bob up and down. You can't see it affecting an aircraft even when you see one close to the ground...but the passengers can feel it. It always feels worse than it really is.

So how dangerous is it?

It is not dangerous. Just keep yourself strapped in tightly and it won't feel so bad, because you will move with the aircraft, instead of a moment after—which always makes it seem worse.

How uncomfortable is it?

It's very uncomfortable in the worst cases. But that's not the same as dangerous. It usually feels bad because the occasional feeling of weightlessness gives you a feeling of falling. Remember, what you feel is not the same as what the aircraft is doing.

Can the aircraft withstand it?

Yes. Easily.

Could you lose control of the aircraft because of it?

No.

Are there different types of turbulence?

Yes there are. They are caused by different things. A jet stream with clear air turbulence normally occurs at high altitude. It occurs when two moving air masses rub edges or collide with each other. It doesn't bounce you up and down like turbulence near a thunderstorm but is more rapid and it rattles and shakes the aircraft. Rough air turbulence throws the aircraft around and it would be hard for the cabin crew to walk around or to serve you.

The fact that the cabin crew suspend their service is no indicator of the seriousness of turbulence—they just don't want to spill hot coffee over you.

When you put your seat belt on, pull it as tightly as you can, then snuggle down into the seat and tighten it again and keep tightening it throughout the turbulence, then you'll move as the aircraft moves. Don't try to resist the movements but go with them, and remember to breathe slowly and deeply.

What's that horrible creaking noise during turbulence, and why do overhead lockers come open mysteriously?

The internal fittings on an aircraft are made from fire-resistant mouldings that are slightly flexible. Because the hinges and catches need to be used easily they have a certain amount of 'give' in them. After all, you don't want to have to spend ages trying to open and close something that is used so frequently. That means that when they shake they squeak, bits rub against other bits, and things move inside the lockers. It all adds to the overall noise level. And in turbulence that's what you listen for, isn't it?—noise to support your ideas of danger.

Why not listen to the music channel instead?

Lockers open because they haven't been closed properly.

Why are there so many unusual noises?

You can't describe them as unusual if they happen all the time, they're not unusual to me; maybe they are just unusual to you.

Spend a moment thinking about the difference between the words unusual, unexpected and unfamiliar. Most, if not all noises on an aircraft are unfamiliar, and quite often, to make matters seem worse, they are unexpected. Any sudden noises cause a startle response; in other words, we jump. Even sitting in a modern aircraft this reaction kicks in. When the wheels go down we aren't given a warning by the crew. It's similar when the pilots have to change speed. There's a sudden changed of engine noise. It's the unexpected and unfamiliar nature of the noises that makes us feel uneasy.

Quite often I have seen what appears to be fuel coming out of the top of the wing during take-off. True or false?

False without a doubt. What looks like fuel or fuel vapour is the condensation forming because of the suction on the top of the wing. It's the same principle as water droplets settling on the taps when you run a bath. Air contains moisture whether you can see it or not...and if you change the pressure or temperature it becomes visible. Don't you remember being a child and breathing out quickly on a cold day to make 'steam' come out of your mouth? We used to call it 'huffing'. I still do it on cold days.

14

What's fuel dumping?

This is the procedure of deliberately reducing the weight of the aircraft by pumping fuel out of the tanks into the air through special valves. You can't do it accidentally because you have to unlock certain switches to allow it to happen.

How quickly can you dump fuel?

Depends upon the aircraft type but it's about five gallons a second.

Why would you do that?

On all flights an aircraft can take off at a higher weight than it can land at because the strain is coming off the wheels, not being put on them.

So if after just take-off you needed to land immediately (say a medical emergency with a passenger) the aircraft would fly to a designated area and reduce the fuel load until the plane was light enough to land. And before you ask me...yes, if necessary it could land without reducing weight.

What are these unusual feelings and sensations you get when flying?

Because you can't always see out and get a reference point, if the aircraft accelerates or slows down or tips its wings or puts the flaps in, you can get feelings of sinking, falling or turning. If our bodies are moved steadily such as in an aircraft gently turning, after a few moments our balancing system re sets. Instead of measuring the turn it says, 'This is normal, nothing is happening I'm steady and I'm upright.'

So when the aircraft returns to the level position your head now tells you that you are turning again.

For example: imagine that you are flying level and the aircraft starts a gentle right turn. You feel the sensation as you move to the right, but after ten to fifteen seconds your system resets and says, 'I'm level.'

If you can't see out or you are in cloud, you will be convinced that you are level. When the aircraft goes back to the level position, your brain thinks it's going from level to the left.

So if the aircraft now really does turn to the left you'll get the horrible feeling that the plane is about to fall over its left wing.

The same effect occurs when it speeds up and slows down. Your brain will send you a message saying that you are climbing or descending.

Just after take-off I notice that the engine noise changes and it feels as if the nose is dipping, and I get the feeling that I'm falling. What's happening?

About three or four minutes after take-off it's quite possible that the plane has reached its first allowed height, usually about six thousand feet. At this point the engine power is reduced to stop the plane from climbing, in addition all aircraft have to limit their speed to about 280 m.p.h. below 10,000 for Air Traffic Control reasons. That means another power reduction has to be made.

Even if you don't know much about the laws of motion you'll know that when you put the brakes on in a car you get thrown forward. The same thing happens in a plane, the difference though is that when the plane is climbing you are leaning backwards in your seat. Because the plane is pointing up in the air to help it climb, you first get thrown forward and then, as the plane slows down, you seem to get pushed forward again. Because you have a restricted view of the outside world, through those tiny windows, you will get a sensation of going down. But you're not...I promise.

I hope my pictures of levelling out, climbing and descending help to explain it more clearly.

The aircraft is:
➤ slowing down
➤ or starting to descend
But what you feel is:
➤ being thrown forward

The aircraft is:
➤ levelling out from a climb
➤ or in turbulence
But what you feel is:
➤ falling

The aircraft is:
➤ taking off
➤ or starting to climb
But what you feel is:
➤ being pushed into your seatback

'What you feel isn't the same as what is happening.'

Do you think that airports are friendly or unfriendly places?

Unfriendly. They seem to be built purely for the benefit of the airport authorities and the airlines. The signs are unfriendly and the procedures make you feel as if you're joining a secret society.

Staff become impatient if you aren't sure what to do next. For instance. What on earth does '...now go immediately to gate 14A on the West pier of the domestic terminal and tell them you're late joiners' mean when you're at an unfamiliar airport?

What does it mean anyway?

I wasn't aware that you had to have a degree in airport geography before you're allowed to use 'their' airport.

If they spent more time and effort on making the place easy to use and less time trying to entice you to spend money we'd all be more relaxed. They don't care if they stress you. They just want to process you.

And don't dare ask anyone to repeat something. Their attitude is that you should have listened properly the first time. If they are in a good mood they will repeat it but at a speed that ensures that you'll learn to listen the next time.

I don't blame the staff personally because there are always too few of them on duty to give nervous passengers a proper service.

Do you think you have endeared yourself to a source of sales for your book?

No. I'm writing this for you, not them. Airports add unnecessarily to the stress that passengers suffer anyway. The trouble is that many airlines and airports are so blindingly smug about their service that they don't believe that they could make things better for nervous travellers.

With the millions of pounds available to them wouldn't it be possible to have a nervous flyers' lounge? Perhaps if passengers were able to register as nervous flyers, they could wait in a reassuring environment and be given help to reduce their anxieties. Is that beyond the realms of human ingenuity?

Meanwhile happy, high yield passengers can go and drink away half the value of their ticket in the executive lounges.

Have a nice day.

Chapter Two

AIRCRAFT

Why are there so many warning lights on the flight deck? Are things always going wrong?

Think of it like this. Modern cars now have warnings when you leave your lights on, if the boot is open, when the engine needs servicing, or if the handbrake is on and we don't associate them with danger.

A warning light to me is a source of information, but to you I suppose the word 'warning' can be a source of worry. Let's call them message lights instead.

Message lights have three levels of importance.

➢ Advisory messages tell you what's going on, for example, the wheels are down.
➢ Caution messages are reminders, for example, auto-pilot is off.
➢ Warning messages say, for example, generator number three has low voltage.

How does an aircraft stay up?

As the plane goes through the air the wings sit on a cushion of 'thick' air while on the top of the wing the air becomes thinner and causes suction upwards. The shape of the wing does that by changing the speed of the air on the top and bottom.

The plane gets air over its wings (airflow) by forward

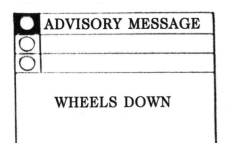

ADVISORY MESSAGE

WHEELS DOWN

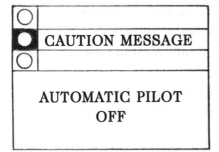

CAUTION MESSAGE

AUTOMATIC PILOT
OFF

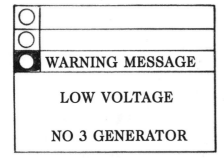

WARNING MESSAGE

LOW VOLTAGE

NO 3 GENERATOR

movement. Incidentally birds make airflow by moving their wings.

But don't tell me that it's a natural thing for birds to fly and not natural for planes to fly. Even after ages of evolution birds still don't fly as efficiently as planes. Have you ever seen a bird carrying passengers?

Compared with aircraft, birds are very inefficient, aerodynamically.

What is a stall? Is it the engines?

No, it's not the engines. One of the most widely misunderstood things about flying is stalling. The wings can stall, the engines can't.

Most of us connect stalling the engine on a car with an aircraft stalling in flight and think it's the same thing. In fact it couldn't be more different. An engine on a car has stalled when it stops running, by some means other than switching it off.

An aircraft stalls if the wings go through the air at the wrong angle. The wings work most efficiently when the air passes over them at the proper angle, which depends upon the speed.

All the pilots have to do is to make sure that the aircraft always goes fast enough to keep sufficient air going over the wings to support the aircraft.

Yes but you might be so busy that you don't notice the aircraft slowing down.

All aircraft have two stall warning systems, the first one is called a shaker and the second one a pusher. If you slow down too much the shaker vibrates the control wheel violently. If you were to miss that, and goodness only knows how you could, the pusher takes

over and pushes the control wheel far enough forward to un-stall the wings by increasing the speed.

How many thousands of feet would you fall?

It wouldn't be thousands, you could recover in as little as 500 feet.

When might I be at 500 feet?

Twenty seconds before landing. Take my word for it that pilots are busy watching everything at that point. Don't concern yourself with airliners stalling.

How does a jumbo jet stay up?

Simply because of its enormous wings. The larger the wings are, the heavier the aircraft they can support. Lift occurs when air over the top of the wing causes suction—more wing more suction. Flying is a simple subject.

What are flaps?

Flaps are the moving parts at the back of the wing that come out for take-off and landing.

How does that happen?

The pilots move a lever in the cockpit. Usually there are five settings for landing which are set one by one as the aircraft slows down. After take-off (three settings) they are selected up as the aircraft gains speed.

Why do they put on flaps at take-off and landing?

To change the size of the wing, they make the wings bigger and more curved...like the wings of a bird when it's landing. There's a nice picture on page 88.

What are ailerons and elevators?

Ailerons are on the back of the wings, out at the wing tips. They make the aircraft bank sideways. The only time you will see them move more than an inch or two is when the aircraft is taking off or landing. This is because the climbing airspeed is less than the cruising speed, so they are less effective; so they are designed to move more at lower aircraft speeds.

The elevators change the aircraft's elevation (they make it go up and down). The elevators are on the back of the tail plane wing. Moving the controls on an aircraft is like moving a steering wheel on a car—the faster you are going the less movement you have to make.

Aileron is one of the most difficult words to say, it's a French word meaning aileron, I'm told.

Here are some wrong ways to say it. Air-ler-on Error-lon Air-lon.

Impress your friends with ALE...LER...RON.

What do the fin and rudder do?

Those are the bits that stick up at the at the back of the aircraft and are painted strange colours and designs on British Airways' aircraft. They act like a weathervane and keep the aircraft pointing into the airflow.

It works in the same way that a yacht's keel does...except it's the other way up...and it's in the air and not the water...but, apart from that, it's the same.

Do all aircraft feel the same when you're flying them?

Modern airliners generally do. The only difference between a light aircraft and a large aircraft is that you have to make allowances for the time it takes for them to change direction and speed but it's no more than the difference between a saloon car and a lorry.

Do you think of how big the aircraft is when you are flying it?

Not really. The pilots fly the instruments and the rest follows, so it doesn't really matter how big or small the plane is that's behind you. You have to think of its size when you are taxiing, of course.

Which is the best plane you've ever flown.

A Tiger Moth.

What is the best flight you ever had?

My first solo flight in a glider when I was sixteen.

What are the tyre pressures of an airliner?

About 150 pounds per square inch. A car tyre is about 30 p.s.i.

How many commercial flights are there in the world in a day?

I can't find an accurate answer to that anywhere. Count the number of airlines in the world add together the number of aircraft they have and multiply by six because that's on average the number of flights each aircraft does in a day. It must be at least 1,000,000. If it's fewer than that you can have your money back.

Chapter Three

ENGINES AND FUEL

How does a jet engine work?

Cold air gets sucked or pushed into the big hole in the front, gets heated up by fuel in the middle, and extremely hot and high-speed air gets blown out of the smaller hole at the back.

Why do planes have jet engines?

Because they are more efficient than propeller engines at high altitude. The advantage of flying at high altitude is that you can be above the weather so the flight is more comfortable (and the view is better).

What about the ones that still have propellers?

You'll find that most planes, except the very smallest actually use jet engines that have propellers on the front of them. This gives them the advantage of shorter take-off and landings. Propellers bite into the air more quickly at low speed so they get the plane up to flying speed more quickly.

What fuel do jets use?

Paraffin which is like the stuff you put in greenhouse heaters. But it's carefully refined, stored and delivered. For instance, you couldn't just take fuel from one aircraft and put it straight into another. It has to be cleaned first.

What's so special about jet fuel?

Remember those news reports in the coldest days of winter when lorries stop because of frozen diesel fuel? That's at minus 10 degrees centigrade roughly. Jet fuel has to stay unfrozen down to minus 40 degrees centigrade. If the fuel starts to get down to that temperature you can warm it up by going faster (air friction) or you can descend into warmer air.

Why would the temperature drop to −40?

In fact the air temperature doesn't drop to that. At very high altitude that's what the air temperature is because the air doesn't get warmed by the ground. The air cools the wings and because the fuel tanks are in the wings the fuel gets colder. Even though the outside temperature is often as low as minus 56 centigrade, the fuel doesn't get that cold because of insulation around the tanks and because the fuel in them is circulated by pumps. Garden ponds that have a fountain rarely freeze completely. It's the same principle.

How powerful are the engines roughly?

If you were to say that most car engines are about 100 horse power, then you could say that most big jet engines are about 70,000 horse power. That's each engine of course. On small business jets they are about 2,000 horse power. A racing car engine is about 800 h.p.

Do you have ignition keys?

No, there is one main switch to turn all the electrical systems on, and then we start the

engines on separate switches. Can you imagine what it would be like if we used keys?

> 'I thought you had them?'
> 'No, you had them last'
> 'Which coat were you wearing?'

Why do the engines take so long to start?

I'm tempted to say because we can't find the keys, but the truth is that it's because the engines are so large. It takes about a minute to start most jet engines.

Do they ever have major faults?

Very, very rarely but for $10,000,000 each you wouldn't expect them to.

Do they get a lot of servicing and checking?

Yes, before every flight the engineers check them in case there are leaks or things have come loose, in the same way you check your car before you go on a journey. In addition, of course, there all the other checks that are performed every three days, each month, year, and when required, a complete overhaul.

Do engines have fire extinguishers fitted in them?

Yes, they do and they are very efficient. Each engine has two.

Do you have spare batteries?

Because the electricity we use comes from the generators and we never run on the battery you could say that the battery is always spare. If needed, the battery would supply enough electricity to fly most aircraft for at least an hour and a half.

What happens if an engine stops?

We land at a suitable nearby airport if it's a two-engined aircraft. A three- or four-engined aircraft can continue to its destination.

One of the interesting things about jet engines is that even if they are not giving power they can still provide power to hydraulic pumps and generators because they are turned by the airflow going through them.

How to you put an engine into reverse so quickly on landing?

Because the engines don't reverse, they don't turn the other way. The reversers just push the air that comes out of the back of the engine forwards instead of backwards.

I visited the flight deck after the captain had said that we were flying at 600 m.p.h. When he showed me the speed indicator it showed about 275. Why?

There are three speeds a pilot is interested in. First and foremost the speed of the air over the wings. That's airspeed. Then the speed over the ground. That's called groundspeed. And then the real speed that he is travelling. That's called the true airspeed.

As an aircraft climbs the air becomes thinner and colder. An aircraft measures speed by the amount of air being forced down a tube. The less air going down the tube, the lower the indication of speed. At high altitude the air is very thin so at any speed there won't be much air to go down the tube. But the wings don't mind, they still get enough air over them to lift the plane because of the true speed.

Why three sorts of speed?

We fly at the proper airspeed to make sure the wings work efficiently at different stages of the flight.

True airspeed is the actual speed through the air.

Groundspeed is used to navigate by. It's the true speed plus or minus the wind effect.

At 500 knots groundspeed, you travel 500 nautical miles in an hour. If it's 500 miles between places you can work out that it'll take an hour to go between the places.

Why do some planes have two engines, some three, and jumbos four?

Before the Boeing 757 was designed, it was thought that engines weren't reliable enough to allow them on two-engined planes flying long routes over water. So the three-engined TriStar and DC10 were developed to reduce the operating costs on those types of routes. After millions of hours of flight the engines were found to be reliable enough to be used on two-engined planes to fly across the Atlantic and other oceanic routes. Modern engine monitoring systems send information to the ground so that health checks can be carried out during flight.

Do two-engined aircraft fly special routes to stay near land?

They used to have to fly a route so that they stayed within two hours' flying distance of an airport. Then it changed to three hours. Now they follow roughly the same routes as jumbo jets.

How much fuel does an aircraft carry?

Most aircraft on local flights will have about 2,000 gallons on board. A long-range jumbo flight might have 40,000 gallons in its tanks.

A 767 which I used to fly would carry about 15,000 gallons of fuel to go to New York, because you need to have some extra in case the weather, or traffic conditions delay you and you need additional fuel to divert if necessary. And the law says that you have to carry some extra fuel (contingency) in case something happens that you haven't thought about.

A 737 from Glasgow to Stansted would carry about five tonnes. For every tonne heavier because of passengers or cargo a 737 would need an extra thirty kilograms of fuel. Ask a lorry driver how much more fuel he uses when the lorry is fully laden compared with when it's empty. Weight has the same effect on a plane's miles per gallon as it would on a lorry's m.p.g.

You just said 'if something happens that you haven't thought about'. Don't you try to think about everything anyway?

Yes, but you still have to have spare fuel for things you haven't thought about. The only time I ever used the extra (contingency) fuel was on Christmas Eve waiting for Father Christmas to land first.

So how much fuel do you carry?

> Enough for the route plus...
> Extra for diverting to another airport plus...
> Extra for holding at the destination plus...
> Extra for things we haven't thought about...

An interesting fact is that if you were to take another 1,000 gallons just for the fun of it, you wouldn't have that extra amount over at the end of the flight. Because it takes more power to carry the extra weight you consume ten per cent of it every hour you fly. So in a seven-hour flight to New York that extra 1,000 extra gallons would be down to about 300 extra gallons.

Actually it would be a little more than this because the ten per cent is of a smaller amount each hour but I only just passed 'O' Level maths so that's how I used to work it out...just to be on the safe side.

Why do you say interesting?

I'm fascinated by planes and to me it is still interesting. Generally, pilots don't marvel or wonder at things; we just accept things as facts.

Now that I'm retired I can return to my childhood wonderment and interest.

Chapter Four

AUTOMATIC PILOTS

What's a blind landing?

A blind landing is a different name for an 'autoland' (an automatic landing). These are landings made in very low visibility. They are flown automatically by two or more automatic pilots working together. But pilots often do 'autolands' in good weather too, for practice. If an aircraft is capable of automatic landings then a pilot on that type has to do three automatic landings every six months to keep his licence valid.

What do you mean by low visibility?

Surprisingly, the conditions when pilots talk about low visibility are much worse than they are to a car driver. Road conditions would be considered bad if visibility were reduced to 100 metres or so. At 100 metres, the roads would be at a standstill. On a runway the conditions are measured by the number of runway lights that are visible (in reality this is done electronically) but of course the lights are very bright and they point exactly along the runway. You know that the fog lights on a car can be seen much further away than the ordinary lights; so it is with runway lights. My idea of poor visibility is very different from yours. I can land my plane with 350 passengers in the back and then not be able to see my way out of the staff car park. But my car doesn't come with millions of pounds worth of autopilot.

Is a blind landing hard to do?

No, because the pilots are not doing anything except monitoring the autopilots. Many years ago I had the privilege of being on the first wide-bodied aircraft to do an automatic landing in conditions where we made the decision to land only twelve feet above the runway. Prior to that the decision to land was made at 100 feet, so it was cutting-edge stuff at the time.

Since then of course things have advanced and the pilots don't make a decision as such, they just land regardless of the visibility. Looking back it was no big deal. We just checked the equipment, pressed the autoland switch and that was that. The 350 people on board didn't get excited and nor did we. What's the point in wasting heartbeats?

Why are there so many delays when it's foggy?

Aircraft need more space between them when doing blind landings so that they don't get in the way of the radio guidance signals from the ground.

But the main reason for delays in bad visibility is that not all airports are equipped with the ground facilities to allow blind landings. In poor visibility the taxiing traffic slows down, bigger gaps are left between taxiing aircraft, so it becomes more and more congested as time passes.

Airports like Heathrow have taxiway lighting systems that show the routings the pilots have to follow, which helps to keep traffic moving. But there are not many airports like that.

What else can an automatic pilot do?

An autopilot can do anything a human pilot can do except take off and taxi. Because taking off is so easy to do there's no help needed. Finding the touchdown point in thick fog would be impossible without help from the autopilot.

Tell me more about them.

An autopilot can keep an aircraft straight, keep it level (height) turn corners, go up, go down, maintain a pre-determined height after climbing, do the same after descending. It can maintain any set speed after going up, in level flight or going down, it can follow a radio beam, can maintain a speed, control a speed, change speeds and remind you of speeds. It can navigate, tell you when's a good time to climb, to save fuel, tell you when's the best time to go down; can land.

It can be connected twenty seconds after take-off and then fly the entire route, land, put on the brakes and keep the plane exactly in the middle of the runway.

You have to disconnect it to taxi to the parking gate though.

Do they keep the aircraft steady?

Yes, they do. If turbulence makes one wing go down, the autopilot will correct for that because it wants to keep the aircraft going in a steady (constant) direction. But the natural stability of the aircraft will help as well.

Tell me about the built-in steadiness of an aircraft.

Pilots would use the word stability. If a wing goes down, the aircraft slips sideways, and causes the lift on the downside wing to increase, which makes it come up again. The lift on the higher wing is decreased so it goes down.

If the aircraft skids from left to right or right to left (like turning without banking) the bit that sticks up at the back acts like a huge weathervane and turns the aircraft back the way it was pointing. If the nose goes up or down, the small tail wing will give a correction to make it level out again. And just in case you're worrying that when I said the aircraft slips sideways when the wing goes down I'm talking about a few inches—not hundreds of feet.

What other safety features and equipment are there on aircraft?

Fire extinguishers, automatic oxygen supplies, lifejackets, life rafts, life cots, standby (spare) instruments, fire blankets, an axe, smoke hoods, fire detectors, smoke detectors, de-icing devices, aircraft avoidance equipment, rate-of-descent warnings, flap warnings, undercarriage warnings, too-fast warnings, too-slow warnings, too-high warnings, too-low warnings, not-working warnings. Open-door warnings, toilet smoke warnings, automatic toilet fire extinguishers. First-aid kits, checklists, handbooks, direct-to-company radio links, engineering assistance, technical assistance, medical assistance. Automatic air traffic control signals. Weather radar. Navigation system warnings, instrument warnings, loud hailers, orange hats to identify the crew. Portable oxygen for sick passengers. Aspirins, pain-killers and medical things I can't tell you about.

And lots of things that I have no doubt forgotten.

The best safety feature is the well trained crew.

And sick bags.

I feel like saying that things must go wrong frequently to have so many warning indicators and safety features. But why are there so many?

That's another difference between the way I see things and the way you see things. A warning light to you seems to be connected with failure whereas to me a warning light tells me that something is working properly. For instance when I turn on the switches that de-ice the wings or engine I get information, not a warning. I suppose the name warning light gives the impression of malfunction; I haven't had to think of it like that previously. Like I said before, I think of them as message lights, not warnings.

What is the advantage of using the automatic pilot?

Being a pilot is not a question of just flying the plane. It has more to do with managing the flight. We use the autopilot to perform low-skill tasks. Flying the aircraft is considered a low-skill task for the autopilot because it doesn't have to think. Meanwhile the pilot can get on with the management of the flight.

Brains are best used for thinking and planning.

It wouldn't make sense to use the skill of a human to do something that a piece of machinery can do. And when the human can't manage because of visibility as in blind landings the autopilot can actually do it better.

Can you fly without them?

A modern aircraft is not allowed to fly without a working autopilot.

Do you trust them?

Yes.

How do you switch them on?

Most airlines use a push button that shows blank if it's off or, if it's connected, says CMD, which means command. It's in command of flying.

Can you override it?

Yes, you can. Because the autopilot controls up, down, left and right, you can disconnect or override one of the controls and leave the other in. Or you can temporarily override a part of the control such as disconnecting the navigation and just steering it by using the direction function.

What happens if it goes wrong?

They don't go wrong nowadays. But if the autopilot has a small problem and is still able to fly the plane it will display an amber-coloured light called a caution. An autopilot caution light means 'take note of what's going on...you might need to intervene later'.

If it's not capable of flying the plane, it will disconnect and make a loud warning noise, and display a very obvious red light that says ' autopilot disconnect'.

You can't miss either.

By the way a small problem may mean that the height control is only working to plus or minus thirty feet instead of the usual plus or minus ten feet.

Chapter Five

ORDINARY PILOTS (HUMAN ONES)

What sorts of people make the best pilots?

The ones that can fly the plane accurately, smoothly, think clearly and stick to the book.

What else do they have to be?

They have to be good team members and have the confidence to speak up when they think it's necessary.

How easy is it to fly a jet aircraft?

With the right training almost anyone who is sensible could learn to fly one.

How many years of training does it take to become a pilot?

Two years to get a commercial pilot's licence and several thousand hours of experience to become a captain.

Do you have to train on each aircraft you fly?

Yes. For a fully qualified and experienced pilot it takes about forty hours of simulator flying and then about twenty real flights to qualify. I almost forgot to mention the two-week ground school where we learn about the technical side of the aircraft. And the examination following it.

Can you fly all the aircraft that you are qualified on?

No. You can only be qualified on one big aircraft at a time. You can only fly one that you have previously been qualified on after completing a refresher training course.

What about women pilots?

Just as keen, just as capable, no differences at all. Most of them are highly motivated and love flying.

Is that all about women pilots?

No. I've taught many women to fly. Some have become instructors and one even became a world-class aerobatics display pilot. None ever became airline pilots because when I last taught basic flying women were not encouraged to become professional pilots.

However, I have had the pleasure of having met several of the wartime ATA pilots. They were the women who were given only basic flying training and then were given the pilots' notes to something like a Spitfire or Lancaster bomber and without even having sat in one before, ferried them from one airfield to another.

The women pilots I have flown with commercially are excellent pilots.

Do pilots ever take chances?

No, and why should they want to? Commercial pilots have to stick to the book. Almost everything that can happen to a flight has been thought about and is written into the manuals. Corporate culpability in the wake of several incidents ensures that airlines

keep within the rules and in turn they make sure that their pilots do.

What does a check pilot do?

A check pilot is someone who observes pilots working in their normal environment and assesses them with regard to how well they apply the company procedures and the law. A check pilot doesn't advise on what training is required to achieve the standard, neither does he give training.

He reports his findings to the chief pilot of his fleet. The Civil Aviation Authorities have access to all check flight reports.

Is that different from a training pilot?

Yes. A training pilot teaches pilots how to fly the aircraft and tests them on emergency procedures.

He reports his findings to the chief training pilot of his fleet. The Civil Aviation Authorities have access to all training reports

What's the point of all that?

Think of it this way. What would be the effect if your driving instructor examined you, as well as taught you how to drive.

The chances are you'd pass because he'd teach you what he thinks is important, and would examine you to the same standard. Someone independent can see different things. That's why the airlines have to do it like that.

How much rest do you have to have before a flight?

An absolute minimum of twelve hours after any work period.

Who are the best pilots—young ones or old ones?

Who are the best drivers? Who are the best at anything? It depends what you mean by best. Old pilots have more experience; young pilots are very good at the actual flying skills and learning new things. Usually crews are made up of one of each, simply because of the experience levels.

In a year how many tests would you have?

These are the tests that all pilots have to pass in one year to stay qualified.

> ➤ Flying skills—normal.
> ➤ Flying skills—emergencies (in a flight simulator).
> ➤ Technical knowledge.
> ➤ Safety procedures.
> ➤ First aid and medical.
> ➤ Two flights under observation (in an aircraft on a commercial flight).
> ➤ Two medical examinations.
> ➤ Human factors' skills.

What happens when you don't get on with the other pilot?

Since the mid-1980s there has been a complete change in the way crews are trained.

In addition to technical knowledge and piloting skills all pilots have to undergo what is called Human Factors training.

Because we're all human, we make mistakes. In the old days, the 'fifties, 'sixties and even the 'seventies, it would have been worth more than a co-pilot's life to point out a captain's mistake.

Human factors' training has changed that attitude. Crews are expected to speak up when they don't agree with things that are being done or if they see things they don't understand. Crews are required by law to brief each other about their duties and actions during take-off, landing, during the cruise and in the event of a malfunction.

Nowadays the captain will insists on hearing the co-pilot's view and during his pre-flight brief will remind him or her of that.

Pilots and cabin crew now have to attend courses on human factors each year as a part of their refresher training.

(What's more, the medical profession are using our knowledge in this area to improve their teamwork skills. Many pilots teach team skills to hospital-operating theatre teams.)

Can you choose who you work with?

Not usually. An airline with more than a handful of pilots and cabin crew would find it very difficult to personalise rosters although most companies try their best to do so.

Do you often fly with the same person more than once?

Even in a big international airline it's surprising how often you fly with the same people.

How many flights can you do in a day?

One, if it's a long one. Two if it's a long one with a short one immediately following it. Or a maximum of six if they are all short flights. Some very small airlines that do short hops on single pilot aircraft can do even more.

But, if you're delayed, with special permission you can extend your duty period but you have to increase the amount of rest you have after the flight.

The rules are very limiting.

If a planned duty is longer than about sixteen hours then you have to carry an extra pilot.

Are you allowed to fly if you are sick?

No. You can't choose to fly if you are feeling ill. The law requires you to be fit for duty.

What about a cold?

No, because the pressurisation effects can't be balanced quickly enough in your inner ear and you could damage your eardrum.

Dentist?

No. Not if you've had any sort of anaesthetic.

Can you be a blood donor?

No.

Can you fly after scuba diving?

No.

Can you fly after drinking alcohol?

No. At least eighteen hours free of duty must follow any drinking of alcohol. Even after a small amount. And that's measured from the time of the last drink.

What about fatigue?

Fatigue is different from tiredness. If you're tired, you can sleep and feel refreshed. Fatigue is long-term and needs a different cure. In cases of fatigue you have to report unfit for duty.

What about food poisoning?

When on duty pilots have to eat different types of meals. That's the law.

Seafood or anything that's likely to cause an upset stomach is not used in crew meals.

Crew-members not on duty still have to eat different meals when they are away from base and staying in hotels in order to reduce the chances of food poisoning.

What could you do if both pilots were incapacitated?

It would be extraordinary if it happened, I've never heard of it. Usually there's a pilot on board somewhere.

When do you retire?

Some airlines retire you at fifty-five, but sixty to sixty-five is the usual retirement age. Some countries (France for example) won't allow captains older than sixty to fly in their airspace. As you get older you may be allowed to fly only as a co-pilot.

How do you take off?

That's a quick change of subject. I normally have hours to prepare to fly.

Select the engine power switch to 'take-off power'; at half-power check everything is normal, at 95 m.p.h. we check that the engines are giving the right amount of power (we don't often use maximum power). We watch the speed increasing until it reaches about 150 m.p.h., depending upon the type of aircraft and its weight, then move the control wheel backwards until the nose comes up and the aircraft lifts off the runway.

You have to keep the aircraft in about that nose-up position until the aircraft is safely airborne. When the altimeter shows that you're climbing, you bring the wheels up, then you adjust the nose position to keep the speed gently increasing. As you pass about 1,000ft above the ground you select the flaps up, one setting at a time until the aircraft is clean then you select the autopilot and have a cup of tea.

Clean—what does that mean?

Sorry, that's pilot talk. It means that the wheels are up inside the fuselage and the flaps are all the way up inside the wing.

Why do you take off power if you want to take off?

When I said we select 'take-off power' the engine doesn't take power off, it sets the engine to 'the power required to take off'. Mistakes have happened in the past because of that expression. We always say 'reduce power' when we want less of it.

How do you know what height to climb to?

The controller who gives take-off permission also allows you to climb to the first height, usually about 6,000 feet. This is decided by the departure route that you are given before you taxi to the runway. After becoming airborne he will instruct the pilots to speak to the next controller who is allowed to give clearance to another height, usually about 20,000 feet. Then eventually, when in contact with the airways controller, he gives permission to climb to the cruising level that is shown on the flight plan.

What happens if the radios stop working?

That happened to me once. You adopt the radio failure procedures which allow you to follow your agreed flight plan all the way to the destination. I flew from Heathrow to Newcastle with total radio failure. We were given clearance to take off and that was the last thing I heard. Afterwards I was told that Air Traffic Control could hear me sending messages and position reports so they always knew where I was and what my intentions were.

Aircraft have equipment that sends a coded signal to the radar controllers to identify individual flights. On this flight I sent the code that said, 'We have had a radio failure.'

When I contacted ATC later on the telephone, the controllers said they thought it was a textbook radio fail procedure because they put into practice all their procedures for keeping other aircraft clear of me and they kept in touch with each other on their telephone links. They loved it because it so rarely happens.

I said that I was a bit anxious at first. Their reply was: 'Yes, we could tell by your voice.' I had an excellent young co-pilot with me who gave me some very good ideas on ways we could try to solve the problem.

When you are sitting there hour after hour what do you do?

We eat and drink. At altitude the body becomes dehydrated so we drink plenty of water. We take short breaks to stretch and have a bit of mental relaxation. And we are also allowed, under certain circumstances, to have a catnap. It's recommended that naps should not be longer than forty-five minutes because the body goes into a deeper sleep which is harder to wake up from.

This is only allowed with the other pilot's agreement, and it has to be done at a time of low workload in the cruise. The other rules are that you have to be awake well before the next period of activity and the cabin crew have to be informed.

The cabin crew are required by law to check on the well-being of the pilots every twenty-five minutes in most airlines.

You must have flying duties too?

Yes, we do. But they are the sorts of things that don't need lots of physical activity so it looks as if we're never doing very much. At least that's what the passengers used to think when they visited us.

Pilots are best used as managers and monitors.

Modern aircraft require managing; that's what the pilots role is now. The automatic pilot flies the plane and we manage the flight. As a resource, pilots are best used as managers and monitors, to keep an overview of what's going on.

During the cruise we check that the fuel consumption is correct, that we are within our required fuel reserves; we monitor the navigation to ensure that we are flying according to the given route. We listen to weather reports. We speak to the company about arrival times, the aircraft's state and passenger requirements. During the flight we notify the company or handling agent about the fuel to be loaded for the next flight, and any operational matters concerning the passengers.

We listen and respond to radio calls, plan and think about our course of action if something were to go wrong, such as a passenger being taken ill.

We prepare for things that could happen but never do.

I spent thirty years preparing for things that never happened. And that's true of most pilots.

Before the descent from the cruising height we spend fifteen minutes briefing for the landing—confirming the route to the airfield, the runway that we'll land on, what the minimum heights we are allowed to go down to at various positions on the arrival procedure.

We also check the taxi route, and how to get to the parking gate.

Does the autopilot do the landing?

Usually.

Is that safe?

That's like asking is your steering wheel safe. It's 100 per cent safe and it's reliable and it doesn't get it wrong. In fact the autopilot could put the plane in exactly the same position on the runway touchdown area ten times out of ten.

And it never goes wrong?

I can only speak for myself but I've never had one go wrong and I haven't heard of anyone having problems. In the old days maybe it happened when multi-autopilot procedures were new. During the landing approach indicators on the flight deck show the status of the equipment. Nothing would happen suddenly without prior indication.

Do you have windscreen heaters and wipers?

Yes, we do; the heaters are electrical like some of the upmarket cars. But the cockpit air circulates around them as well. The windows never mist up. The windscreen wipers have fast or slow settings and we have rain repellent that stops the rain sticking on the screens.

How far can you see from the flight deck?

If the visibility is good about 120 miles at cruising height.

How do you do a good landing?

A good landing starts with a good approach and a good approach starts with good preparation and planning. A good landing is one where the aircraft touches down at the correct point on the runway at the correct speed at the correct nose up position and with checklist complete.

Or did you mean a soft landing?

What's the difference?

A good landing to me is a safe one like the one I've just described, where everything is done properly according to the book. A jumbo jet is easy to land softly and correctly. It has such enormous wings that as it gets near the ground a great cushion of air forms between the wings and the runway which helps the aircraft to touchdown softly. Certainly it's a nice feeling to have achieved a soft touchdown, but don't make assumptions about safety from 'hard' landings—nor make assumptions about what you think is a hard landing. On wet runways it is much better to do a firm landing so that the water is squeezed from between the tyre and the runway to give a good grip; then you can slow down more quickly.

Maybe the question should have been how do you land an aircraft?

An aircraft usually lands at its lowest possible speed so that it uses the least amount of runway and having landed hasn't enough speed to 'fly' into the air again—or what you would probably call a bounce.

To fly at the lowest speed possible the wing flaps have to be extended to their maximum. This you will remember makes the wings as large as possible.

You have to have the wheels down and locked in position.

After leaving the holding area an aircraft will normally be lined up with the runway about ten miles away from the airport at a height of 3,000 feet.

At 2,000 feet the pilots will lower the undercarriage and start the final approach checklist.

As it gets closer the crew extend the flaps more and more until at 1,000 feet they will be fully extended.

The speed will be set according to the weight of the plane. The lowest speed before the flaps are used would be about 230 m.p.h. and the lowest speed at touchdown with all the flaps would be about 130 m.p.h.

The checklist ensures that the aircraft is set to land or, should it be necessary, to be able to climb away from a missed approach (not because they've missed the runway, it's an Americanism that we use to mean any approach that doesn't end with a landing).

If you are flying the aircraft manually, that is not using the automatic pilot, about three miles from landing, you make a gradual change from looking inside the cockpit to looking only outside the cockpit when you actually touch down. As you get nearer to the runway you have to keep a check on the speed and the rate of descent. You look at the runway and the lights that show you the correct approach angle.

As you get closer and closer you try to keep everything steady. If you need to change the power setting you try to anticipate it so that you change it as little as possible. With the aircraft at a steady angle it's easy to fly. If you fiddle with things the aircraft is harder to control accurately.

For example, if the speed reduces, a slight increase in power will put it right. If it's been steady throughout the approach it may have been caused by a drop in the wind speed so you have to be ready to reduce the power again when the speed is right.

The nose position is vital. If you push and pull the nose up and down unnecessarily the descent will change and the aircraft will quickly depart from the perfect approach path. So gentle adjustments are needed.

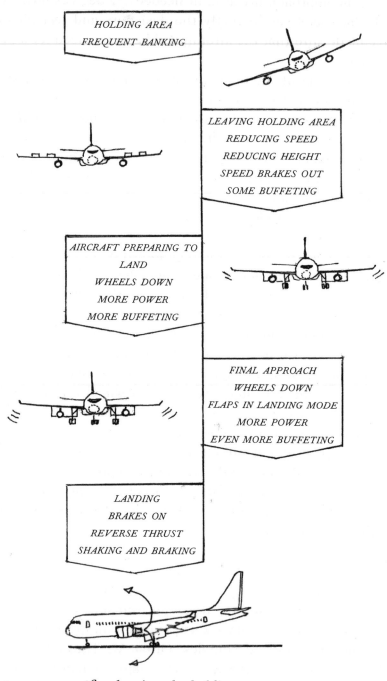

HOLDING AREA
FREQUENT BANKING

LEAVING HOLDING AREA
REDUCING SPEED
REDUCING HEIGHT
SPEED BRAKES OUT
SOME BUFFETING

AIRCRAFT PREPARING TO
LAND
WHEELS DOWN
MORE POWER
MORE BUFFETING

FINAL APPROACH
WHEELS DOWN
FLAPS IN LANDING MODE
MORE POWER
EVEN MORE BUFFETING

LANDING
BRAKES ON
REVERSE THRUST
SHAKING AND BRAKING

After leaving the holding area...

On the approach my aircraft needed 2½ degrees nose up and with the speed set correctly the designers and test pilots will have made sure that the aircraft will be well placed for a perfect touchdown.

On big aircraft the pilots are much higher above the runway than the wheels so the wheels touch down sooner than an inexperienced pilot would expect. So it's a question of flying by the book and by the numbers. The automatic voice system calls out the heights above the runway. '100 feet' is the first call. You have to look towards the far end of the runway, then look back at the touchdown area.

You have to check inside the cockpit for speed, descent and attitude.

At '50 feet' you look at the touchdown point.

At '30 feet' you check speed and descent close the thrust levers, and start to raise the nose gently, while look up the runway, if you keep moving the control wheel backwards the aircraft will gradually settle into the landing position.

At '10 feet' wait for the touchdown, and you've kissed ground before the passengers even know you've landed. As the speed reduces you have to move the control wheel forward to lower the nose wheel to the ground gently, check the automatic brakes engage and ask for reverse thrust.

At about 95 m.p.h. we disengage reverse thrust and turn off the runway and do the 'after landing checklist'.

With any luck the co-pilot will say, 'Nice one, skipper,' and you say, 'Thanks for your help.' A safe landing is always the result of good teamwork.

Then what happens?

The checks after landing are done from memory because it's important that both pilots keep a good look out on the ground for other aircraft and vehicles. Often Air Traffic Control give permission to do something in the form of a condition: 'After the departing Lufthansa on Gate 6 you are cleared into the Charlies for Alfa 5.' That means 'when the Lufthansa aircraft has taxied away from Gate 6 and is out of your way then you are cleared to enter the parking area named Charlie and park on gate number A5; do not expect any more instructions.'

Just before that famous call 'doors to manual', we check that we are about to park on the correct gate and, if we haven't already stopped one of the engines, we do it now and then taxi very slowly to the park position. We stop an engine as we taxi in order to conserve fuel.

Why is that bit done so slowly? You think you're parked and then it creeps forward another inch…it doesn't seem worth the trouble.

Airport space is limited. Modern passenger aircraft are big. So the pilots have to put the aircraft in an exact position. As the aircraft approaches the terminal jetty or gate, marker boards become visible to help the captain park in the correct position. He has to align two markers sideways and two in front so the aircraft stops on its correct spot. The jetties have to reach everything from a jumbo jet to a small inter-city hopper so parking even a few inches out means that the jetty can't get into its proper position.

So a jet weighing a hundred tons is, as you can imagine, quite difficult to manoeuvre at low speeds and if you stop too soon it takes a lot of power to move it and then, having moved it those few inches, it has to be stopped again.

The brakes are designed to stop the aircraft from anything up to 200 miles an hour so we have to use them very carefully to stop smoothly from 2 miles an hour.

Then what?

We do the shut-down checks, fill in the technical log, complete all the other paperwork gather our briefcases, coats, headsets and hats and get off.

…And go home.

Chapter Six

THE WEATHER

What is a crosswind?

A crosswind is a wind that blows across the direction that an aircraft is wanting to go whether it's on take-off, landing or when en route. There's no limit to the amount of crosswind that you are allowed when cruising but for taking off and landing it's about fifty m.p.h. maximum.

What is a tailwind?

A wind that blows from behind the way an aircraft is going or wanting to go.

What is a headwind?

A wind that blows towards you.

Can you have both at the same time?

You can have a wind that's blowing at an angle to you, which will cause a crosswind and a tailwind (or a headwind).

What makes weather?

Weather is made up of air.
    And the air has three qualities: movement, temperature and

moisture. The weather depends upon how hot (or cold) the air is, how much moisture it contains and if it's moving or not.

How does the weather happen?

If you imagine a town surrounded by fields and the hot sun beating down it's easy to see that the town will heat up quicker than the fields because it's made of thicker things like houses and cars and concrete. As they get hotter they heat the air over the town. When it gets hot enough the air suddenly breaks away and rises like a bubble, and it keeps rising until it cools to the same temperature as the air surrounding it. (Things cool down as they go up.)

What happens to all the moisture that was in the bubble of warm air? It appears out of the air, not as rain, but tiny water particles that are so light that they continue floating upwards in the current of air. In fact they become clouds. These are the fluffy ones called cumulus. If there's a lot of moisture in the rising air the water particles join up and fall as gentle rain…upon the earth beneath.

What's the difference between a fluffy cumulus, a shower cloud and a thunder cloud?

The only difference is in size. But to become different sizes they need more moisture in them to start with and the temperature of the surrounding air has to be such that the cloud goes up a long way.

And finally, to turn into a thundercloud the air has to be unstable. And that means that even if a bubble of air is getting cooler as it goes up it still stays warmer than the surrounding air.

Have you ever been struck by lightning?

Yes.

What does that feel like?

Fortunately I was in an aircraft at the time and all that happened was that there was a loud bang, and we carried on normally. The noise is a bit like sitting inside a tin dustbin while someone hits it with a garden spade. It's noisy and makes you jump.

Being in an aircraft is safer than being in a dustbin though.

No sparks?

No sparks, just a bit of paint knocked off the nose and a dent the size of a small egg.

Quite undramatic.

Did it tilt the aircraft?

No, but remember that near thunderclouds the air is bouncing you around anyway so it would make a passenger think that the lightning was making the aircraft move.

So what actually happens and why doesn't the plane crash?

What happens is that lightning, which is static electricity, normally jumps from the clouds to the ground. If something gets in the way, like an aircraft, it hits that instead and doesn't continue to the ground.

And you're safe from electrocution in the same way as a bird is when it's sitting on a power line.

The inside of an aircraft is an electrical cage and electricity can go along the outside of it but not inside. It discharges through things that look like artists' paintbrushes on the wing tips.

And it doesn't and cannot crash because nothings actually happens to the aircraft.

There is a phenomenon where some small amounts of electricity gather together in the form of a ball and travel through the aircraft before going out through the 'paintbrushes'.

I'm told that if someone tells you about it they should use the word plasma somewhere in their explanation. If they don't, just ignore them.

It too is harmless.

What makes electricity form in clouds?

The particles of air brushing against each other cause friction, and if you've ever caused friction between your shoes and a brand new carpet you'll know how much static electricity can be made. That spark you get between your finger and the metal thing you touch is a miniature form of lightning

Earlier you said near thunderclouds, not in thunderclouds?

That's right: aircraft are not allowed in thunderclouds. At cruising height most companies require pilots to stay away from the centre of them by twenty miles. The bumps in the air extend a long way from the thunderclouds. All passenger aircraft carry airborne radar which show areas of turbulence on a screen. To make it even easier to understand, the different areas are of turbulence are shown in different colours.

Sometimes the weather looks good and we can't fly and other times it looks awful and we do fly. Why?

A pilot is only interested in four bits of weather.

> What's it like for taking off?
> What's it like for landing?
> What's it like at cruising height?
> And is any of it going to change?

For taking off?

> A pilot must be able to see far enough along the runway to steer straight.
> The wind must not be more than about fifty m.p.h. directly across the runway.
> If there is snow or ice on the runway it must not be deeper than a certain amount according to aircraft type.

Once again your idea of good and bad weather won't be the same as mine.

For landing?

When I started flying the weather for landing had to be very good compared to the weather that aircraft can land in now.

With modern autopilot systems we can land in much more limiting (worse) weather and in greater safety too because autopilots can't make errors of judgement. They do it all by electrical numbers.

We know about changes in the weather from the airport broadcasts that are available twenty-four hours a day.

Do hailstones only come from thunderclouds?

No, any cloud that has strong up-currents could cause hail to form and it is more common than you would imagine. Of course by the time they have fallen from the clouds and hit the ground they have usually melted and we just feel them as rain. Hailstones are frozen raindrops.

Is fog just thick cloud on the ground?

Yes. We call it fog rather than cloud because it forms near the ground and under certain conditions.

If the air is warm and moist and the ground suddenly cools down as it does on a cloudless night the air cools down and is unable to contain the moisture so it condenses out as water droplets.

Sea fog formation is slightly different because it results from the cooling of warm moist air as it crosses areas of cold water.

How thick does fog have to be to stop you from landing?

The best equipped aircraft and crews can land in any thickness of fog.

Do air pockets really drop you thousands of feet?

Well, apparently so, according to some of my guests to the flight deck. There are no such things as air pockets: you can't have nothing in the middle of something. Not in air anyway. Air pockets are the biggest myth since radio ventriloquists, and food tasting on the tele.

What really happens to you in an aircraft is that it feels as if you are dropping...a bit like going over a hump back bridge at speed. The faster you go the more you feel the bump. That's what happens when you hit a bump in flight. And then you have to come down again on the other side; that's what you think is the air pocket.

How does the air make bumps?

Find yourself a river and watch the water flow by. Most of it goes by smoothly without a ripple. But have you noticed what happens to the smooth flow of water if it goes around a rock or a log sticking out of the water? The water makes ripples and changes direction slightly according to how fast the water is flowing and how big the obstructions are in the river.

Things like mountains, hills, continents, cliffs, woods, buildings, towns, cities, and trees all make air bump around and change direction. Have you noticed that it gets more bumpy nearer the ground on a windy day when you're lucky enough to be flying. That's because the wind is hitting the buildings and making the air swirl around.

Close your eyes in a car when you're a passenger and see how much turbulence from the road you go through without giving it a thought.

And if you've ever been on a funfair ride what's the difference?

'Turbulence; did you hear that? The pilot just said turbulence again.'

What is it with the word turbulence? It doesn't mean danger it just means uncomfortable.

Strap yourself in tightly. Breathe deeply and slowly and keep pulling your seatbelt tight..

Can you take off in rain?

Yes, you can, because rain has no effect on the aircraft at all. It doesn't stick to the wings so it doesn't affect the aerodynamics. It doesn't affect the engines either. Our screen wipers give us excellent visibility along the runway regardless of the amount of rain.

You said that you were interested in the weather at cruising altitude. Is that for passenger comfort reasons?

Partly. When we have an accurate forecast of the weather it means that the cabin crew can decide the best times for serving meals and hot drinks without the fear of spilling them or having to stop the service. Areas of clear air turbulence are very accurately forecast nowadays and we can often arrange the

route to avoid them, it also means that we know how long we are likely to be bumped around for.

We need to know what the winds are like at cruise altitude because it changes the amount of fuel that we carry.

So you don't always get the same miles per gallon (kilometres/litre)?

No.

If your car does thirty miles to the gallon and you are going to see your aunt who lives ninety miles away you'll need three gallons to get there whether you go today or tomorrow.

In an aircraft the wind will change the journey time. And winds at 35,000 feet or thereabouts are usually 70-80 miles an hour and often 100+ m.p.h.

Here's a bit of fun.

Let's imagine that we're on an aircraft that uses 1,000 gallons of fuel per hour.

We're going on a flight of 2,000 miles

We cruise at 500 m.p.h.

Flight time will be 4 hours.

Fuel needed will be 4,000 gallons

Now imagine on the way there the wind is 100 m.p.h. against us, that means that instead of travelling at 500 m.p.h. over the ground we are now travelling at 400 m.p.h. At that speed it will take longer (because we're going slower)...in fact it will take us 5 hours.

That's an extra hour's fuel and that's another 1,000 gallons needed.

So this trip needs a total of 5,000 gallons

Coming back is not so bad because in addition to our cruising speed of 500 m.p.h. the wind will push us along at another 100m.p.h making our speed on the journey back of 600 m.p.h.

At 600 m.p.h., we are travelling at 10 miles each minute

So to do 2,000 miles will take 200 minutes.

Total flight time home again is 3 hours and 20 minutes which is 3,000 gallons for three hours flying plus 333.3 gallons for the 20 minutes. Total fuel needed 3333 gallons.

The difference in time between the outbound flight and the inbound one is 1 hour and 40 minutes.

So the two flights would carry very different amounts of fuel.

The difference is 1667 gallons. So one flight might be able to carry more passengers and cargo than the other.

You mentioned about when the weather changes, is that important?

Yes, it's the most important thing we need to know. We want to know what the weather will be when we arrive at our destination, not what it's like as we are leaving. On long routes the forecast is very important. In the course of even a short flight the weather can vary enormously...and of course throughout any flight we collect weather reports for our destination airport as well as the diversion airports on the way.

Knowing what the weather will be like when we plan to land is important because if we know the weather is improving we can leave for our destination before the weather is good enough to land, confident in the knowledge that by the time we arrive it will have improved.

A simple question. Why do I feel so unsafe during turbulence?

A simple question with a long answer I'm sorry to say.

A few explanations first: there are six main feelings or sensations connected with turbulence, up and down, backwards and forwards, heaving and going sideways. I'll deal with them in turn.

UP AND DOWN

Which feeling do you prefer—going up or going down? In a lift (elevator to my American readers) although we get a 'heavy' feeling when the lift sets off to go up, it's still a better feeling than that awful one we get as the lift slows down to stop at a higher floor. What's happening is that you keep on going up and the lift slows down. That's why you feel as if you are coming off the floor, EVEN THOUGH YOU ARE GOING UP YOU ACTUALLY GET A FEELING OF FALLING.

The strange thing is that you get the same feeling when a lift starts to go down. You stay where you are and the lift falls away from you until you start falling and catch it up. Whether you are slowing down from going up, or speeding up before going down, the feeling is the same.

During turbulence the aircraft is going up and down just like a lift does but over a much shorter time and height. What you don't know is whether the next movement is up or down so you don't have the chance to prepare...you don't know what the next feeling will be.

It's worth remembering that we associate a feeling of falling with danger. Few people hurt themselves jumping up and hitting their head on the branch of a tree but many of us have hurt ourselves falling from a branch.

In turbulence, the aircraft is alternately going up and down; well strictly speaking it might do two small ups and one big down, or two small downs and a big up. Whatever it does it certainly doesn't feel normal. What's more you have no control over it so it doesn't feel safe either.

BACKWARDS AND FORWARDS

Which do you prefer to do in a car—accelerate quickly or brake sharply? A car salesman will tell you enthusiastically that a car will reach 60 m.p.h. in 6.8 seconds but he won't tell you that it'll stop from that speed in 4.6 seconds even though it's a much more impressive figure. We associate slowing down with danger because we assume that something must be impeding our progress. Slowing down is an uncomfortable feeling compared with going faster.

In turbulence the aircraft is flying in gusty conditions. When the aircraft encounters a gust, which will last about one or two seconds, it slows down very slightly. You feel this as being thrown forward in your seat.

HEAVE

Do you know that awful feeling called heave? It's a feeling well known to anyone who has been on a boat or who sails or who has been tipped out of a chair. It's the feeling where you go forward up and over. If you think of a small boat going up one side of a wave then just before it comes down the other side it tips forward, then you know what heave is.

GOING SIDEWAYS

Going round a corner with someone who drives too fast is another uncomfortable feeling. You get thrown from one side of the seat to the other. Because your head is heavy and can pivot easily on your shoulders it moves quicker and further than your body so you become giddy as well.

Now combine going up, down, forwards backwards side to side and heaving in a very short period of time and keep those movements going for more than a few minutes and what have you got?

Turbulence?

Not quite because the effects of turbulence is more like, up backwards, heave, up sideways down, sideways, heave, down, up forwards, forwards, sideways, down, backwards, down, up, sideways, forwards, sideways, heave. A short break and then more up backwards, heave, up sideways down, sideways, heave, down, up forwards, sideways, down, backwards, down, up, forwards heave. Add a bit of shake rattle and roll and noise and a bit of anxiety and I have almost answered your question.

Tighten your seat belt and remind yourself that whatever it feels like to you it isn't dangerous.

I feel airsick.

Chapter Seven

AIR TRAFFIC CONTROL

What does mayday mean?

Mayday stands for *m'aidez* which is French for help me.

Mayday is the international signal for distress. If a pilot makes a Mayday call, all other aircraft have to copy the message they hear and assist in sending it to a ground station. No one else may use the channel for communication.

How many times have you sent a Mayday message?

Never. I've not even heard one let alone sent one.

How good are Air Traffic Controllers? Do you trust them?

ATC controllers, almost without exception are excellent. They have years of training. A controller at major airports will have had years of experience in supporting roles before carrying the full responsibility of controlling. They will act as an assistant for a period while they get accustomed to the procedures in force at an airport before they work on their own.

Some smaller airports might allow you to visit them and see what happens there.

How do Air Traffic Control 'talk you down'?

They don't. However nice it would be to think that there's someone on the ground free of pressure to land the aircraft, it is sadly... untrue.

But they can give help with the navigation. Their radar picture and map is so accurate they know exactly where an aircraft is at all times so no aircraft really needs navigation equipment.

So why don't Air Traffic Control do the navigation of all aircraft?

Because it's not their main job. ATC organise aircraft so that aircraft on the same route don't get too close to each other and give each aircraft a clear space in which to climb and descend. Like their title says, they are controllers of traffic.

When I fly to Athens from London how does the arrival airport know when my aircraft will arrive, and how does my pilot know if he is at the right height when he gets to the airport?

In the same way that your tour operator can organise a coach to meet your flight to transport you to your hotel, so departure messages are set to all the countries that your flight will go over. Nothing happens by chance or without planning.

If an airline has a regular flight to Athens every Monday, then stored in the ATC computer will be all the information for that flight:

> Aircraft type
> Take-off time requested
> Speed at cruising height
> Requested cruising height
> Requested routing...because some countries are cheaper to fly over than others
> Alternative landing airport

On the day of the flight the airline 'activates' the flight plan, by confirming with ATC that the flight is operating. ATC will make 'space' for that flight and all the countries on the route, on receipt of that message will make space too. Unlike a railway where the signals can stop a train when the next bit of track is occupied the air traffic system has to organise everything before it can let anyone take off.

What happens if one aircraft catches up the one in front?

It will be asked to slow down. But don't forget the radar controller will see it catching up and intervene if they get closer than about fifty miles.

Is that why they have to give their cruising speed on the flight plan?

Yes. Then Air Traffic Control at the departure airport can let faster aircraft take off before the slower ones if they happen to be ready to take off at the same time.

So what happens to all the space that's made available for my flight to Athens if we take off late because a passenger gets lost in the terminal?

They save it for a while then give it to someone else who might want the route or part of it. That's what an ATC slot time is. They come into force when airports and airways are so busy that ATC can't swap routes and take-off times so easily.

Although it may not look busy where you are it may not be your part of the route that's congested.

What about crossing the Atlantic where there is no radar?

Aircraft give very accurate position reports to the controllers in Shannon and Northern Canada who are in contact with each other. They plot where aircraft are on the routes.

Aircraft going in opposite directions aren't on the same route because if the wind blew in a direction that helped one aircraft it wouldn't be helping the other.

So if the ones going East are flying over one part of the Atlantic the ones going West are somewhere else. This makes controlling them easier and is why radar coverage is not essential. This is called the Organised Track System.

Who decides all that?

The air traffic controllers and the weather forecasters.

So the routes are constantly changing?

Not constantly. They are reviewed and revised every twelve hours or so according to the weather. Each morning the routes are decided and notified to all airlines who then choose the ones that suit them. When there are significant changes in the winds they are re-organised.

What does holding involve and is it difficult?

An aircraft has to hold when there is not enough clear space ahead of it to continue. Usually ATC will say to an aircraft, 'Expect to hold at Dover,' and sometimes they will add, 'you may reduce speed now if you wish.' Sometimes, to keep aircraft apart and to reduce holding times, aircraft are asked to reduce speed en route.

Approaching an airport, aircraft are never closer to each other than about ten miles. On the final approach to the runway, when all aircraft are travelling at about the same speed, they are about three miles apart. Remember that the slower they go, the closer they can be to each other without danger because they are the same

time away from each other. It's like racing cars getting closer at the corners.

Why do we usually go into the 'holding stack' just before landing?

It's a system of waiting prior to landing. It becomes congested near an airport because aircraft arriving at London from Hong Kong won't have been so accurate in the estimate of their arrival time as a flight from Paris. And even if it's only two minutes different someone will have to have his or her landing time changed. How many times on a train have you waited outside a station before going the last few yards to the platform? The railways don't call it 'holding on the track'; in fact they don't name it because it isn't anything special.

Perhaps humans feel differently about it because we associate waiting with being stationary.

And just in case you're tempted to ask, pilots do not walk round in circles with their arms extended when they're waiting in a queue; they stand still just like normal people.

What does it look like when other aircraft are going round with you?

To us at the front it looks spectacular because we get such a good view of other aircraft and we can work out when we are likely to move down the 'stack'. But when you're in the passenger cabin other aircraft can look very close...and when your aircraft turns it can look as if other aircraft are changing height. But don't worry, everyone stays strictly at their allocated height until cleared (given permission by Air Traffic Control). The aircraft are on autopilots which fly within an accuracy of ten feet or so.

The difference in heights in the holding areas is 1,000 feet vertically from each other and aircraft don't change heights until the preceding aircraft is clear of his previous height by 200 feet. It takes about two minutes to change levels.

While I was relaxing in the garden recently I saw a small plane doing acrobatics. Then I saw a jumbo jet flying in the same place. Should that be allowed?

It isn't allowed…and they would not have been in the same place although it might have looked like it. The small aircraft would have been allowed to fly up to a certain height and the jet would not have been allowed to go below a certain height. And, in case you're worrying, there's a gap between the two heights.

What precautions are in place to minimise the chance of terrorists hijacking aircraft?

Any information regarding security should be publicised as little as possible. Locked cockpit doors are a line of defence of course, high quality security at airports is another, public awareness and intelligence-gathering are less spectacular but powerful influences on deterring terrorists.

What I can say is that the world-wide authorities governing air transport work together and constantly review their security.

Terrorists gain advantages when we leave unattended bags around and when we are uncooperative with security workers. They watch for breaches in security processes and use them to their advantage. Every passenger can do something towards security by sticking to the rules.

Chapter Eight

IN THE COCKPIT

Did you like having visitors to the flight deck?

Yes, because judging by the faces of people who have visited, most didn't know what to expect. I always likened it to being Father Christmas watching grown-ups opening their presents. Since 11th September, cockpit visits are prohibited.

I haven't been in a flight deck. What is it like?

The cockpit is divided into two identical sides—the captain's and the co-pilot's side. We have the same instruments which always show the same information. Sometimes we can set our navigation information differently but speed and height and direction information is always shown.

Everything else in the cockpit we share; that means all the switches that control engine starting, fuel pumps, cabin signs, anti-icing, electrics, radios, navigation systems, hydraulics and air-conditioning. These are positioned above our heads on the 'overhead panel' or on the console between us.

(Another thing we share are the wages. The captain gets ¾ and the co-pilot ¼.)

We each have a control wheel, rudder pedals and a steering wheel for taxiing.

But the thing that makes it look really complicated and which everyone asks about is the overhead circuit-breaker panel. The circuit breaker panel is like the fuse box where electricity comes into your house. Whereas at home we have one fuse for, say, upstairs lights and another for upstairs wall sockets, an aircraft has a fuse for every single item on board.

Here's an interesting and fascinating list of things that need circuit breakers or fuses:

> Radio 1, Radio 2, nav system 1, nav system 2, lav flush rear, lav flush front, seat-belt signs, no smoking signs, landing lights left, landing lights nose, attitude indicator left, right and standby. Airspeed indicator left, right and standby, air data computers 1,2 and 3. Wheels up light, wheels down light, wheels up and down warning lights not working light. Hydraulic contents, pressure, and flow lights 1,2,and 3. Anti-ice left right and wings.

I'll miss out the other 800 or it'll seem repetitive.

But the reason for all those breakers is that if the slightest thing goes wrong with any system it just trips off without affecting anything else on board.

Clever but expensive. Expensive but safe. Safe and sure.

I noticed you said that 'if something goes wrong'. Does that mean you have to fly without whatever it was?

No. The standby system takes over.

So if you've always got a backup, the systems must pack up frequently?

No, but it helps to explain why flying can be so expensive because even the backup systems on board have to meet the same rigorous maintenance standards as all the other equipment.

I notice that when the engines start up the lights go on and off and there are a lot of unusual sounds. Why?

An aircraft can supply its own electricity and air-conditioning on the ground, from a small jet engine, at the back of the aircraft by the tail. It's called the Auxiliary Power Unit (APU).

But the APU is much more expensive to run than the electrical power supplied by the airport authorities. They supply power through a ground connection which may be a diesel-engined generator on the back of a lorry. So airlines usually choose to have the lorry supplying electricity to the aircraft rather than its own APU. The problem is that lorries don't fly too well, so at some stage they have to be disconnected.

Because generators have to connect to the aircraft's electrical system very accurately there's always a delay between an engine starting and the generators connecting. That's when the lights go on and off.

You've missed out the unusual sounds.

So each time the power supply changes the aircraft measures how much electricity there is available and turns things on and off accordingly.

High-powered things like air-conditioning, fans, electrical hydraulic pumps, and galley power are automatically turned off and on during the start sequence so that the power can be directed to starting the engines. And they're all noisy bits of equipment, so you will notice them going on and off.

That seems like very poor design if this all happens each time you start the engines?

It may seem to be but the time is used to test and check that everything works properly.

What would you do if the windscreen cracked?

Nothing. Each section of the screen is made up of three layers of toughened glass so if one breaks the other two maintain the air pressure in the cabin.

In the cockpit who knows what to do and when?

No airline can carry passengers until it has an approved set of procedures. And that applies to engineering, boarding procedures, re-fuelling procedures, and almost anything else you can think of.

In the cockpit, where the two pilots may never have met, let alone ever having flown together, it's vital that they each have defined jobs to do. These are known as Standard Operating Procedures and every airline has their own. Normally they are based on the manufacturers' recommendations.

They lay down clearly things like which pilot takes off, which pilot operates the switches, changes the flap positions, and who talks to Air Traffic Control.

Does that mean that a co-pilot never does a take-off until he's a captain?

No. Even though the procedures are strictly laid down, they do allow for the pilots to change roles. Normally the captain will fly the first leg (flight) and then the co-pilot flies the next and so on. It's up to the captain's judgement and the rule book to decide whether the conditions are suitable for the co-pilot to fly the aircraft. Usually the captain will be the more experienced of the two anyway. Sometimes the rules demand that the captain flies the aircraft, for instance when doing a blind landing or when the crosswind is stronger than that allowed for co-pilots.

Describe a normal flight

The pilots would normally meet an hour before the flight and check the weather reports, the engineering record of the aircraft and all the relevant Air Traffic Control information for the route. They would decide how much fuel to load and then go to the aircraft, meeting the cabin crew on the way. They discuss the expected flight time, the weather conditions and anything of special interest to the cabin crew. In turn, the cabin crew will advise the pilots of the numbers of passengers travelling and if there are unaccompanied children or disabled passengers needing special assistance. The operating crew go about their separate duties, one checking the cabin, the other the flight deck.

Normally both crews would do what are called Safety Checks. The cabin crew checks will involve checking all their passenger safety equipment and the condition of the cabin interior. Meanwhile one pilot will check the inside, while the other one will check the outside of the aircraft. That is, they make sure that all the switches and things are in the right positions before they do the normal checks.

In the cockpit, for instance, they will check that the under-carriage selector is in the down position, that the parking brake is on, that all the electrical circuit breakers are set in their correct positions. One of the pilots will check the technical log for the aircraft and see how much fuel it landed with and if there are any snags.

Any snags. What does that mean?

Problems that the previous crew encountered or things that aren't working.

Then what?

They carry on reading to see if it's been repaired.

And if it hasn't?

They get an engineer to fix it or check their manual to see if they can fly without it.

Fly with something not working?

Every piece of equipment on the aircraft is listed in a manual called The Dispatch Manual. In there it will say if an item has to be serviceable or if it can be accepted as 'an allowable defect'. If it is allowable then very stringent conditions are imposed about the use of the aircraft.

All the items in the manual are considered and approved by the manufacturer, by the aviation authority and by the airline.

But what about something in the cockpit?

Same thing applies. But the captain always has the right to refuse to fly with an allowable defect. Just because the book says he can accept it doesn't mean that he must.

What do you do next on this flight?

So, having done the safety checks, we do the checks that get the aircraft ready for flight. We scan the cockpit, that is we look around the cockpit in a systematic way and set everything into its correct position and check instruments for the right indication or we set it to the right value. For instance, the altimeter measures pressure to show height so we set the known pressure and see that it shows the airfield height. The speed indicators should be showing zero and things like oil gauges show the correct amount of oil. It takes about seven minutes to do a complete scan. After that we set the navigation equipment for the route we're allocated.

The pilot checking the outside will make sure that there are no oil leaks under the engine (yes, I know an engineer has done this as well) and that there's no ice or snow on the wings. He'll check that all the places which measure pressure for the altimeters and speed indicators are clear of blockages. He'll check the brakes and the general condition of the outside of the aircraft.

That keeps him busy for about as long as it takes the other pilot to set up the cockpit. When they meet up again they get information about the take-off conditions and departure route and set it into the flight management computer. When all that's done they read the 'before start checklist' and make sure all the important things they did from memory have been done properly. Then the refueller gets on board and shows the pilots how much fuel he's put in the tanks. He adds it to the amount that he thought was on board. The pilots check it against what the last pilot recorded plus what the refueller thinks he put on and if all that agrees the captain signs the log for the fuel and checks that it is what he ordered and what he needs for the flight.

There's a lot of checking going on, isn't there?

Yes, there always is. No one trusts anyone...in the nicest way of course.

Have I mentioned the just-in-case factor?

Then what?

Time to sign the ship's papers, welcome the passengers and ask for start-up clearance.

How do you start the engines?

We always check with the ground engineer that it's safe to start. Jet engines take in so much air that any debris, including people, could be sucked into the engine if they are too close. And they blow out so much hot air that the area behind the engine has to be clear too.

So if an aircraft is pushing off its stand behind you, then you can't start up?

Not until he's clear.

Is this what helps to make delays?

Yes.

You were talking about starting the engines.

Yes, so if the engineer says, 'You are clear to start engines,' we read through a short checklist including things like 'handbrake on' except that we say 'park brake set'. We check that the fuel pumps are running, (they're automatic on a car) and that the doors are closed and all the passengers are seated. The switches we use to start the engines are like the round switch on a microwave. We select 'ground start' and air is blown through the engine to turn it and when it's at a high enough speed we turn on the fuel switch which allows fuel into the engine and within a minute the engine is running.

Why does it take so long to start? A car starts immediately?

Because it's big...simple as that. A car has a different type of engine.

What are the checklists when you've done that?

As you'd expect the next checklist is called the 'after start checklist'. We check that the air-conditioning is turned on, control wheel set, hydraulics and electrics working, flaps set for take-off, taxi light on, anti-icing if needed, automatic brakes set. And then get taxi clearance.

Automatic brakes?

Yes the brakes go on automatically during an aborted take-off so the pilots can concentrate on just keeping the aircraft pointing straight down the runway. At any time the aircraft system can sense the position of certain controls. If the flaps are in a position used for take-off and if the power is increased beyond a certain amount the aircraft will say to itself 'the pilot wants to take off'. If subsequently the pilots reduces power the aircraft will say to itself 'the pilot has changed his mind...he doesn't want to take off'. On sensing that, the system will say 'if he doesn't want to take off then he must want to stop...so I shall put the brakes on for him'.

And it can apply the brakes harder and quicker without skidding the wheels than any human pilot could.

Quicker?

Yes because we would have to take our feet off the rudders which we use to assist steering and lift them onto the brakes. The brakes are on the rudder pedals.

When taxiing, how do you know which runway to go to?

When pilots get on board one of the things they do is listen to the information service. This broadcasts the weather conditions the take-off runway and any special information that may be important like a change of the take-off runway or if a taxiway is closed for repair. Knowing which runway is in use means the pilots can see which departure procedure they will have to use for their route.

How do you know which way to go?

We always look at the taxiway charts just to be certain but when you've been to an airport a few times you get to know the usual routes. And they have markings on the ground showing things like 'Taxiway 3' or, at airports like London, ATC will say 'follow the greens to 27L' which means exactly what it says. 'Follow the green taxiway lights and they'll take you to the Runway Two Seven Left.' Green lights along the centre of the taxiways are turned on by the ground controller to take you all the way to the runway. Red lights across the taxiways mean that you have to wait—just like traffic lights but built into the taxiway.

What about in thick fog?

You can see the green lights in thick fog. At many airports ground radar is so good that controllers know exactly where all the aircraft are and can guide them if necessary.

OK. Then how do you take off?

When ATC say we are clear for take-off we confirm that we are on the correct runway and we ensure that the take-off checks are complete. The other pilot confirms by saying 'take-off checks complete' and we line the aircraft up along the runway. When the aircraft is straight on the runway all we have to do to apply power, by pushing the power levers forward or by pushing a button about the size of one of these keyboard keys I'm using now, and thousands of horse power are gently released to push us along the runway. The computers work out the exact amount of power required, and adjust things according to the temperature and the pressure around the engine. We keep the aircraft straight by using the steering wheel and the rudders until we get to Vr (rotate speed) and we pull back on the control wheel until the nose lifts and we fly.

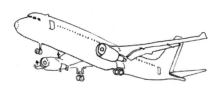

Chapter Nine

GROUND CREW

When the captain says he's waiting for the traffic dispatcher or the ship's papers what does he mean?

The traffic dispatcher is the person who is responsible for preparing the legal documents for the flight and presenting them to the captain before flight. The flight cannot go without the papers being signed by both the dispatcher and the captain.

One of the legal requirements before an aircraft is allowed to take off is for the number of passengers to be recorded, along with the amount of fuel and cargo that is on board. Having all the passengers in the back or the front of the cabin may cause the aircraft to be out of balance.

So the fuel and passengers have to be distributed in a way that keeps the aircraft in balance for the whole flight.

Is it serious?

Yes and no. It's a safeguard, remember that the aircraft can still fly when it's out slightly out of balance.

The ship's papers?

The captain can't fly the aircraft until he has confirmed that the aircraft has been loaded properly and he needs to know what sort of cargo is on board. If it's your pet cat or alligator, he can turn on the cargo-hold heaters to keep it warm. We don't warm the baggage during flight; that's why it's often so cold when you pick it up at arrivals.

So why do we have to wait for the dispatcher sometimes?

Because it may be necessary to take extra passengers or fuel because of the route or weather and sometimes we take cargo that was not taken on an earlier flight. We may also wait for transiting passengers from flights that arrive late. And they have to be accounted for legally. The dispatcher's target is to get the flight to leave on time. He is responsible for the co-ordination of everything affecting the departure.

Waiting for the dispatcher is not a reason to start worrying.

Is their job more stressful than yours?

I wouldn't do it for twice what a pilot earns.

Do check-in staff have a part in flight safety?

Yes. Check-in staff have to check on the fitness of people to fly— that is that they're not drunk or acting suspiciously. They have to be vigilant in all respects and ensure that security procedures are enforced. Which they do...even if you don't see them doing it.

What's the refueller's job?

The refueller's job is vital and highly skilled. They don't just put the right amount of fuel on board. They check the quality of the fuel, its temperature and its density. They ensure that the fuel is put into the correct tanks and advise the dispatcher and captain of any discrepancies. They are not petrol pump dispensers by any means. They are trained in the safety aspects of fuel delivery and fire precautions. To prevent static electricity causing sparks the refueller has to bond the aircraft to the tanker before refuelling starts. He does this by connecting a length of wire to the aircraft from the tanker.

Can you refuel with passengers on board?

Yes you can as long as exits are available and clear of obstructions and there is a crew-member near each exit. This is in case of a fuel spillage.

By the way, the 'no smoking' signs must be on, and the 'seat belts fastened' signs must be off.

What about the people who bring the food to the aircraft?

The caterers. They have to ensure that the correct trolleys are boarded that they are stowed properly and locked into position. They have to know about the galley and its equipment on each aircraft they work on. There are no unskilled staff involved with the departure of an aircraft. They, like everyone with access to aircraft, have to display identity cards.

What happens to the aircraft overnight?

Engineers put the aircraft 'to bed' as they say. They turn off all the equipment, put all the switches into safe positions, put the brakes on and close any valves and access panels that are open, which otherwise might encourage stowaways and others. They put locks into the wheels to make sure that, when they 'wake' the aircraft in the morning, the wheels can't be retracted accidentally. They put streamers on all these things to show that they need to be removed before flight. Then they put blocks under the wheels to make sure it can't move and kiss it goodnight because engineers just love their aircraft.

Chapter Ten

IN THE CABIN AND LOOKING OUT THE WINDOW

Why do the crew tell me what to do in an 'emergency' if they almost never happen?

Just in case. The whole of the aviation industry works on the 'just-in-case' factor.

In reality is it worth listening to the safety briefing?

Yes, it is.

I always listen to any safety briefing. I always read the safety card. I never talk during the safety briefing in case someone else wants to hear it too. Out of simple courtesy and politeness I do not continue to read newspapers or magazines during the safety briefing.

I look at the person giving the safety briefing so that they know that at least one person on board is interested in what they are saying.

When we listen to the safety briefing, do we feel that we are tempting providence to be prepared?

Is a motorcyclist more likely to fall off if he or she is wearing a safety helmet?

Are yachtsmen more likely to fall into the sea if they wear life jackets?

Are you more likely to have a car accident if you wear a safety belt?

Of course not...but if things were to go wrong they'd be in a much better position than someone who hasn't bothered.

What do you think of passengers who don't listen to the safety briefing?

It can't be that they're all stupid. I think there must be an underlying reason like embarrassment, or maybe they want to look sophisticated and, above all, maybe they think it's irrelevant to them. Whatever the reason though, they are behaving stupidly, and they endanger other passengers. I'd like cabin crew to have the authority to chuck people off if they talk or distract other passengers during the briefing. Not dealing with bad behaviour sends a signal that the briefing doesn't really matter.

Why do the crew dim the lights for take-off and landing at night?

So that your eyes can adjust to the dark conditions quickly if you had to leave the aircraft quickly.

Is the wing moving up and down?

Believe it or not the wings are supposed to move like that. If the wings were absolutely stiff you would get bumped up and down more than you do already. Because the wings move rather than the whole aircraft, you get a smoother ride. They work in the same way that springs act on an old-fashioned baby pram or the suspension on a motor car. Imagine being in bed and being pushed along a cobbled street. Which would you prefer? To be on a stiff wooden slatted bed or a nice sprung interior mattress?

In flight the engines move, should they do that?

Yes, they should. They're far less likely to be damaged when there is a bit of give in the structure rather than if it were rigid. Most structures have a bit of give in them. Remember the Eiffel

Tower sways in the wind and that's over a hundred years old, so it's not a new discovery.

Why doesn't the engine vibrate like a car engine?

First, if you spent ten million dollars on a car engine it probably wouldn't vibrate either, and if you looked after it as carefully as we do aircraft engines, then it wouldn't wear out either. It's a different type of engine; the parts of a jet engine just go round. The parts inside a car engine go up and down.

Why are there gaps in the wing when we take off and land?

They allow air to flow between the flaps and wing to keep the air flowing smoothly; when the air flows smoothly the wing can make more lift.

The difference in speed between when a aircraft is taking off or landing and when it is at cruising speed is about 500 miles an hour. When the aircraft flies slowly it needs bigger wings to support the weight of the aircraft so parts of the wing unfold from inside the wing structure to make the wing size larger. They are stored inside the wing like the leaves of a dining-room table that are revealed when you wind the table open—except on a wing the extra bits come out at the back rather than the ends. And they're not made of wood.

What's that screw thing going round when the flaps come out?

Exactly what you said it is. It's one of several screw jacks that unwind the flaps. If you've ever had to change a wheel on a car you have probably had to lift the car on a screw jack. Do you remember as you wound the handle around the wheel jack got longer and the car got higher? On an aircraft they get longer and push the flaps out. They pull the flaps back in by turning in the other direction

What are all those other bits on the wing?

Those other bits you can see moving on the wing are the speedbrakes, which disturb the smooth airflow and help the aircraft to slow down and/or descend. At the very end of the wing and tilted upwards is a winglet that keeps the air from spilling off the end of the wing and directs it across the wing instead. The ailerons are positioned at the back of the wing out towards the tips and are used to bank the aircraft.

The flaps at the back of the wing near the cabin push the airflow down at low speed to increase lift.

Wings, by the way, are built in one piece and the cabin is connected to it. In other words there isn't a wing each side and the body in the middle. That's why wings can't and don't fall off.

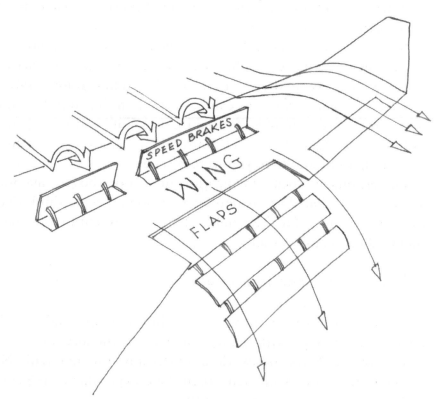

Flaps, speedbrakes and ailerons.

I'd feel safer with a parachute—why don't airlines issue them?

It's a highly skilled process to use a parachute; there's more to it than reading a card with simple instructions on.

You might feel safer with one but what's the reality? Parachutes sound like a good idea but I'm sorry to say quite impractical. If each passenger got out in four seconds it would take twenty minutes to deal with 300 passengers. An aircraft would travel at least sixty miles in that time. You'd never gather them all up in time to put them on the next flight. What about my grandmother, she's 108 next year?

What about ditching in the sea?

Very few aircraft have had to ditch and of those that have, most have been fairly successful.

If this were to happen, the crew have procedures to follow.

All trans-oceanic aircraft have several life rafts that are carried in the doors or near them. They are fully equipped for survival at sea for as many people as can be carried on the aircraft. They have protective canopies, first-aid equipment and emergency radio transmitters. If you had to use one I think that you'd just be settling in by the time you were rescued.

Life jackets are located beneath your seat on the aircraft. You should check that there is one for you, some people think that they pay so much for their ticket that they are entitled to steal them. Check yours is there.

Why do they say 'doors in automatic'?

And the other thing they say is 'doors to manual'. Both comments are to do with the normal exits on the aircraft.

It's not the doors that work automatically; the automatic bit is when the doors are opened—then the escape slide is triggered and passengers can escape down them.

When you are getting on the doors are in manual. They can

be open and shut without anything else happening.

As the pilots start the engines while the aircraft is being pushed off the jetty, the captain or engineer asks the cabin crew to set the 'doors to automatic'. The doors are now 'armed.'

Once this is done the escape slides will deploy if the doors are opened.

After landing when the aircraft approaches the disembarkation point the captain calls 'doors to manual'. When set to manual opening them does not trigger the escape slides. The crew open the doors and you get off.

While we are on the subject of doors, can they open in flight?

Do you mean could someone open them deliberately or could they just come open somehow?

Both.

No to both.

Why not?

Because the doors are too big to go out through the hole that they fill. When the doors on an aircraft open inwards they fit like an ordinary door in your house. You can only open your doors at home in one direction because the builder fits a bit of wood on one side that stops the door opening the other way. So as you close the door it stops against the piece of wood attached to the doorframe, it can't go through the opening. Just like a plug can't go down the plug hole.

In addition, when the aircraft is pressurised, the force on the door to keep it closed is about half a ton of force on each square foot of the door. At home that would be about seven or eight tons of force. Try opening a door under those conditions. So they can't be opened from the inside in flight.

On aircraft which have doors that open outwards, bars extend as the lever moves to the closed position to prevent the door from opening.

If there's so much pressure on the door it could push its way through the side of the aircraft?

No, if you look at the area around the door you will see that it is reinforced.

What are all the noises that you can hear on an aircraft?

There are lots of reasons for them. The fact that the aircraft is going through the air at anything between 120 and 600 m.p.h. will make a lot of wind noise. When the wheels or flaps go down they disturb the smooth airflow and cause noise. When, for instance, you open your car window as you go along the motorway the noise level increases enormously. It's not the wind coming in the car that makes the noise, it's because the air is not flowing smoothly over your carefully designed car.

And what about those jet engines blowing all that hot air out of the back at nearly the speed of sound…that's noisy too.

When the undercarriage goes down the hydraulic pumps run to maintain pressure. They make a noise.

There is a lot of noise from the air-conditioning. If you think of the noise from you car blower/fan when you turn it on to de-mist the windscreen, imagine how much bigger the fans are on an aircraft and how much air they have to pump through the aircraft.

However well the cabin is insulated, it will be optimised for cruising flight so when the engines are running on the ground the sounds they make will enter the cabin.

When the pilots select the flaps to the take-off setting you can hear the motors running that drive them into position. Because the undercarriage (the wheels) is designed to absorb the shock of landing it is designed to be quite stiff; when you taxi over the concrete taxiways the noises and bumps are sent straight to your ears and bottom.

When the wheels go down for landing they have to lock into position like a door catch so the wheels have to go into position quickly to travel over it, and then stop suddenly as they lock into position. When we put the wheels up or down we want them to stay there hence the bump and the bang. If you want to fly with the minimum of noise it's a glider for you or if you're happy with a bit of noise try a hot air balloon. When it comes to jet passenger aircraft you'll have to put up with a lot of noise.

Chapter Eleven

QUESTIONS FROM PEOPLE I INTERVIEWED FOR THIS BOOK

SUE'S QUESTIONS

If there was a fire on one engine, could the aircraft fly on and for how long?

Yes. It could fly for as long as it's got fuel on board, and because it started with enough fuel to get to its destination that's how far it could fly.

Is there an automatic sprinkler system that would douse the flames?

Yes. Each engine has two fire extinguisher bottles; the procedure is that if the fire warning continues after the first extinguisher has been set off then thirty seconds later the other fire bottle is discharged.

The fire warning is a bell and a red light on the switches that control the engine. You can suppress the bell but the lights remain on until the fire is extinguished.

Even if the aircraft is a two-engined one it can still fly on without danger. However, international law requires it to land at the nearest suitable airport.

An aircraft with more than two engines is allowed to continue to its destination.

Going through bad turbulence, how safe are you?

You are completely safe. If you're in the rear of the aircraft the turbulence seems worse than if you're sitting over the wings, because you're furthest away from where it all balances. You will be more comfortable if you have your seatbelt fastened securely. The aircraft is built to withstand forces far beyond those you'd ever encounter in turbulence.

Could the engine fall off?

No. But it's designed to come off in extreme circumstances to protect the wing. For example if the engine were vibrating and shaking so much that it could damage the wing then it would detach under the strain.

They are perfectly safe and secure under all conditions including the most extreme circumstances. It's the 'just-in-case' factor again.

What would happen if someone used a laptop computer or a mobile phone?

The rules and the technologies are constantly changing. At the moment there are on-board phones that are compatible with the aircraft equipment and of course are perfectly safe, but using your own is not allowed.

International and certainly intercontinental aircraft have terminals for laptops so they're safe to use. But not during take-off and landing. Always check first with the crew.

Where is the best place to sit?

I think over the wings is the least bumpy in turbulence. In front of the engines is quietest.

Next to a window in front of the engines is the best view.

Behind the engines the exhaust causes a heat haze and it blurs the view. Sit at the back if you want to get to the loos easily, an aisle seat if you want to get up and down from your seat or you enjoy being disturbed a lot.

The correct answer is the captain's seat.

How safe is the autopilot? When is it used?

Modern autopilots are totally reliable. When they are needed to perform automatic landings at least two have to be connected and working properly. All electrical equipment like autopilots have a thing called BITE installed. That stands for Built In Test Equipment, it allows the equipment to check itself while it's working and if it goes outside prescribed limits it sends a warning and disconnects. That's why you have to have at least two for an automatic landing (and normally it's three).

If the aircraft landed on the sea would there be enough time to get out before it went under?

Yes. Landing on water is such a rare event, but those that have 'ditched' spent enough time afloat to allow people to get off. Fuel of course is lighter than water so that would help to keep the aircraft afloat. They are designed to float with the doors above the water line as well.

How much training do pilots undergo after getting their wings?

A commercial pilot's licence requires a private licence plus another 200 hours of in-flight training. An instrument flying licence takes another forty hours.

A type rating course takes forty hours of simulator training plus five hours on the real aircraft doing circuits and landings. Then

before an airline would accept a newly qualified pilot as competent he'd do another forty flights learning to fly on the routes. Then there are the flight tests to be passed.

The short answer is a great deal.

How often are aircraft given safety checks?

Before every flight.
Every three days.
Every year.

And then they're pretty well taken to pieces and rebuilt about every three years or so. Different manufacturers have slightly different rules.

How often do cabin crew do refresher training?

Cabin crew do about three days' refresher training each year. This will include training on normal safety procedures, fire fighting, first aid, a technical test and human factors training. Before their flights most airlines require their crews to have a question and answer session and discuss possible scenarios that might occur on board.

What sort of qualifications do cabin crew have to have?

I don't know what the minimum qualifications are, but I was on a flight once where I was the least qualified academically. The senior cabin crew-member had a degree in law; all the cabin crew had 'A' level passes and each one of them was fluent in at least one other language.

A story says that a cabin crew-member once inadvertently dropped something on the floor during a flight. While having to struggle around the passengers' legs to retrieve everything one passenger said, 'Don't you wish you'd worked harder at school now?'

Cabin crews have amazing amounts of patience, self-control

and tolerance as well as technical knowledge. They all have training in first-aid skills.

If you were to see them during refresher training you would be very impressed with their knowledge and skills.

Why aircraft are so expensive?

Because every part is manufactured to very critical standards. Don't forget there's an enormous amount of testing and checking to be done throughout its production and prior to passenger use.

When an astronaut blasts off in a rocket he's on the top of a pile of contracts that have probably gone to the lowest bidder. Your aircraft has been built by the people who have submitted the safest specification.

Can you take a used bit from one aircraft and use it on another?

Yes. But used aircraft parts are not the same as finding something in a breakers' yard where you might pick up a dodgy second-hand starter motor. It's not like trying to fit a part from a Ford Escort onto a Vauxhall Cavalier. Parts are carefully maintained and catalogued throughout their lives. Every bit of maintenance work is recorded; every time a part is fitted or removed it is recorded on its 'personal history' sheet. The records will even show which mines provided the ores to make the metal ingot which the parts are made from.

So how do they know about the condition of a spare part?

When parts of an aircraft are overhauled the process is very carefully monitored, recorded and checked. One engineer does the work, while another checks that the work has been done properly. All this has to be done according to the manufacturers' manuals.

How often does an aircraft have a ten-thousand-mile service or equivalent?

At six hundred miles an hour it wouldn't take long to do 10,000 miles, would it? (Sixteen hours and thirty-six minutes in fact, which is about a day's work for an aircraft.)

Maintenance is scheduled by airborne time, not aircraft mileage.

So the answer to your question is that aircraft are maintained all the time. Additionally after a number of hours depending upon the importance and how much a part is used it will be checked or replaced.

Every three years or so it will be minutely inspected and every so often it will be taken apart almost to the last nut and bolt.

What about just before a flight? Does it get a check then?

Before a flight the captain will inspect the aircraft's log book to ensure that the maintenance schedule is up to date and signed for. Then he will make his own inspection of the exterior of the aircraft. And before the captain inspects the log, an engineer will have checked and signed it to confirm his own pre-flight check and to confirm how much fuel and oil is on board.

PAULA'S QUESTIONS

How hot is the air coming out the back of a jet engine?

About 500 degrees centigrade.

Is that what causes the white smoke out of the back when you see a plane high up?

Yes, it's like the warm air you breathe out on a cold day. When you follow another aircraft at high altitude you can see that the air from the wings is spinning the exhaust round in circles. And the circles of spinning white water vapour get bigger and bigger as they expand into the atmosphere. It's a wonderful sight.

If you are in a plane and you look up, you see the sky, if you look down, you can see the ground. What's in between you and the ground?

It's sky, I suppose. But we normally think of sky as being above us. Who am I to argue with John Lennon?

How thick is cloud?

You can't measure thickness of cloud in terms of what it feels like, because it's just moisture. However we can measure it in terms of how far you can see through it, how bumpy it may be inside it and how close it is to the ground. The Red Arrows aerobatics team flying in close formation can see each other when they go into cloud.

Do you have one fuel tank like a car?

Most aircraft have multiple tanks—two in each wing and one in the area between. They can hold nearly as much fuel as the plane weighs when it's empty. Put another way, when a large aircraft takes off at its heaviest, nearly half the weight of it is fuel.

Why, when you watch a jumbo jet take off, do the wings look as if they are bending upwards?

Because they are. Imagine that you are at one end of a plank of wood and a friend is holding the other end. Sit a child on the plank in the middle and let her or his feet rest on the ground. Now gradually lift the plank until the child is off the ground. How much does it bend?

Now find two rugby players and sit them on the plank. If you could lift them how much would the plank bend then? Quite a bit more, I think. So the heavier a plane is when it takes off, the more the wings bend.

Many years ago I was told that the wingtips of a fully laden B52 bomber flex (move up) sixteen feet from being stationary to taking off.

What maps do pilots use on a flight?

On almost every modern aircraft maps have been replaced with flight computers. These contain all the navigational information for the aircraft on any of the routes it flies. A large international airline will buy world-wide information from a supplier, then have a licence to divide it into local routes—European, Middle East, Pacific, North Atlantic, or whatever it needs.

These databases are updated monthly. The engineers input current information by plugging their wires into a terminal and upload information in a matter of minutes. An aircraft will always have two sources of data, the current one and the old one, or the current one and the one that's about to come into force.

But they still carry a selection of paper maps—just in case. Soon aircraft will be paperless. All the information about the performance, navigation, weight and balance will be available electronically.

Does or did one map cover the entire route?

No and the database is in three bits—leaving, travelling, and arriving, that is departure, en route and arrival information. The maps will contain information like the lowest altitude that you should fly at to remain 2,000 feet or so above the highest object covered by the map, whether it's a building, radio mast or mountain. The map will show names of all the airways (e.g. Romeo Twenty-three), the places where you have to report your position, and the directions of the airways.

For landing and taking off, they will show the heights that you should be at in certain positions and the routes in and out of airports. On the landing chart it will show the route you should take to the runway and height to climb to and the route you should take if you have a missed approach. This height will always be lower than the heights of departing aircraft so that they don't get in each other's way.

And they go in different directions?

Yes. There's no guesswork or chance in flying. Everything is prepared and thought about before it happens.

Why doesn't the pilot say that he's about to bank the plane?

Because it would interfere with his concentration if he had to, and of course it happens so often that he'd spend his life talking to the passengers. A bus driver doesn't tell you each time he changes gear. Banking is normal to the pilot.

Why is the plane banked for so long sometimes?

Because if you banked steeply at cruising height the forces on you at 600 m.p.h. would be quite high, so to reduce them the aircraft turns very gently. In fact, to do a complete circle takes over a quarter of an hour. And if you started a turn over the middle of London it would cover half of Surrey, nearly all of Sussex and a large part of Kent. The diameter of a turn at 600 m.p.h., taking a quarter of an hour to do, would be about fifty miles. Halfway round a turn started over London you'd be over Brighton.

Sometimes things appear out of the top of the wings just as the aircraft feels as if it's shaking itself to pieces?

These are called the speedbrakes. These things come out from the smooth surface of the wing and upset the smooth flow of air over the wing. At the manufacturer's factory a team of experts is given millions of euros or dollars to design the perfect wing. Meanwhile in the same factory another team is given millions to make it imperfect by designing a speedbrake.

The speedbrake reduces lift and increases resistance and is used when you want to descend quickly or if you want to slow down quickly. All the pilot has to do is to pull a lever and the flat panels come up to cause resistance to the airflow. This makes the plane shake. I explained this to a young boy who was on the flight deck who said that in that case, they should be called slow brakes not speedbrakes.

I wrote to Boeing and I'm waiting to hear from them.

How does ice affect aircraft?

If ice is on the wings or tail plane it upsets the smooth flow of air and reduces the amount of lift the wing can make. Aircraft have to be completely clear of ice and snow before they take off.

So how do you get rid of it?

The engineer will arrange for a de-icing rig to spray the aircraft with a fluid that will remove ice or snow and prevent it from settling on the aircraft. If you think an aerosol can of de-icer is expensive, de-icing fluids for aircraft cost about a pound a gallon. In a real freeze-up in London many years ago I was the co-pilot of a flight when we used several thousands of gallons to de-ice a TriStar, before going to Paris.

I've been on a flight where I have seen ice on the front of the wing and eventually it has just melted. Did the pilot know, do you think?

Yes, he would have known. Most aircraft have an ice detector. It's a small, loose, but streamlined device that sticks into the airflow from the side of the nose. Normally it stays in position because of the airflow. But if ice forms on the detector it gets out of balance and starts to wobble (that's why it's loose in the beginning). When it wobbles it sends a message to the pilots saying, 'Ice detected.' Then the pilots would switch on the de-icing equipment which sends hot air or turns on an electrical heater to melt the ice.

Some aircraft procedures require ice to form before the de-icers are turned on.

Ice in flight forms on the front of wings, engines and tailplanes.

Ice or frost on the ground settles over the entire aircraft. Aircraft are not allowed to take off with ice or snow on them.

How steeply is an aircraft climbing after take-off?

As you know by now there are two views of everything in a plane, the pilot's and the passengers'.

The passengers will want to know what the angle is and that could be 20 to 25 degrees nose up. The pilot will want to know the rate of climb in thousands of feet per minute and that typically might be 2,000 to 4,000 feet per minute. He'll want to know that in order to work out how long it will take to reach a particular height. So if Air Traffic Control say to the captain, 'Can you be at twelve thousand feet by Brighton?' he can work it out. (Or he'd get the co-pilot to work it out for him.)

What's the difference between altitude and height?

Strictly speaking, height is the height above an airport, and altitude is the height above sea level.

In real life though, we refer to the height of a mountain not the altitude of it. In aviation when we refer to the height of anything, other than the aircraft, we mean its height above mean sea level.

CHARLOTTE'S QUESTIONS

What would the pilot do if all the engines failed?

The pilots would refer to their 'all engines failed' checklist and carry out the procedures.
First to control the aircraft.
Second to navigate the aircraft.
Then to restart the engines.

Why might all the engines stop?

There might be an unnoticed fuel leak from a tank that is being used.
Fuel contamination may have occurred.
Fuel may have frozen.
Volcanic dust may have extinguished the engines temporarily.

How often does it happen?

I have only ever heard of that happening twice in my life. Both continued to safe landings. And the checklist has been written for the 'just in case' scenario, not because it's something that's likely to happen. How many millions of flights have there been in my lifetime of flying? Two incidents...from all those millions. One was fuel starvation and the other the result of volcanic ash.

How much fuel can a plane hold?...How far will that take the plane?

It depends upon the design of the aircraft. A jumbo can hold 150 tonnes of fuel. That's sufficient fuel to fly non-stop from London to Japan. I think that converts to about 45,000 gallons.
Few aircraft need the fuel tanks to be full for a flight. Because

the wings have to be there and you can't put passengers in them, the manufacturers fill the spaces with fuel tanks. There's no point in having an empty space in the wing. Usually the pilot can have as much fuel as he wants.

But do you fill up your car boot with things just because you've got the spare space?

How do you keep the plane balanced?

The aircraft has natural stability and the passengers and freight are loaded within the limits of the design.

If the aircraft were to be loaded so that it had a tendency to fly nose heavy the tailplane at the back would have to be set to pull the nose up to the level position and that's inefficient because it cause unnecessary resistance to the airflow. We try to fly with the tailplane set to the most efficient angle.

Have you ever carried a very heavy bag of groceries in one hand and nothing in the other? It's much easier to carry two bags with half the shopping in each. That's like a balanced plane.

How can you see where you're flying when it's dark?

We only ever navigate and fly by looking at the instruments so whether it's bright sunlight, a foggy day, thick cloud or a dark night we're looking at the instruments. When it's a clear day we look out for other aircraft as a precaution, but nowadays the aircraft electronic avoidance systems maintain clearance from other aircraft.

We don't have to look out of the window to navigate.

How much weight can a plane hold?...Do you have fewer people on the plane if they're all fat?

If we had fifty sumo wrestlers on a small short haul aircraft which has a limited range of weights (unlike a jumbo which can be empty or carry 500 people) then that would be taken into account. After all, they're likely to be a little heavier than fifty ballerinas from the Bolshoi Ballet.

How do planes stay in the air?

The wings develop lift to support the aircraft while the engines make it travel through the air. All the time it's moving it'll stay flying. As the air travels over the round top of the wing it causes suction. Under the wing a cushion of thick air supports it.

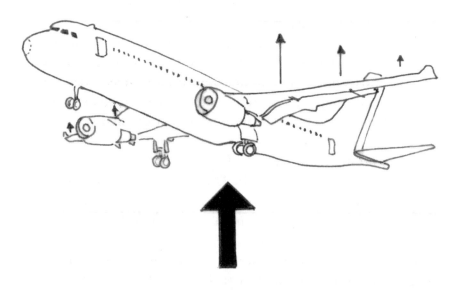

"...suction on top, a cushion underneath..."

What would happen if there was a fire inside the plane?

The cabin crews are trained to deal with it. They know that certain fires need certain types of extinguishers. You wouldn't for example squirt a water extinguisher on to an electrical fire...you'd use carbon dioxide. They know that to fight an oven fire you don't open it to look inside; you just open it enough to get the extinguisher nozzle in, then discharge it.

Their procedures are:

The person that finds the fire fights it.

Then the next on the scene becomes the co-ordinator, then the third cabin crew person becomes the communicator, in order to inform the pilots about the situation.

Then the pilots acting on all the information will decide what to do.

Elsewhere inside the plane, like in the cargo hold, there are automatic smoke and fire detector systems. The toilets are fitted with fire and smoke detectors. In the early days of non-smoking flights, many passengers who popped into the toilets for a quiet cigarette were discovered when they triggered the alarm.

Are co-pilots less qualified?

Not always. Some co-pilots may be new to the company and have to wait for a vacancy for promotion. I have flown with co-pilots with enormous amounts of experience, some as test pilots, flying instructors, and one who was a test pilot teacher. They don't come much more qualified than that.

How long do pilots train for?

The correct, but smart sounding answer, is all their careers.

Do all cabin crew have first-aid training?

Yes, they do and they are trained
to a very high standard and they
are tested every year.

Does the climate affect the performance of an aircraft, i.e. does it use more fuel to take off/land if the weather's hotter or colder?

Yes, the weather conditions do affect the performance.

The hotter the day or night is, the thinner the air is. The thinner the air is, the less of it there is to go over the wings or through the engines, so they don't work as effectively. So we either give it more power for take-off (remember we usually use less than maximum power for take-off) or we take off at a lower weight. Airports in hot climates, or at high altitude, have very long runways anyway.

With the increasing use of booking plane tickets online, how are you able to calculate the weight going onto an aircraft if you are not able to see the passengers...? Would you have to turn passengers away if they were all on the heftier side?

They all have to check in before the flight so if the Sumo wrestlers or the Bolshoi Ballet turned up, someone would notice. Otherwise all passengers are assumed to be of a similar weight. But it's on the high side for safety's sake. The answer to the last part of your question is yes, if the aircraft was above its maximum allowed weight. And of course there is the option of weighing the passengers individually.

MARTIN'S QUESTIONS

How do instruments work?

An altimeter works by measuring pressure. On the ground pilots set the local pressure and the altimeter shows the height of the airport above sea level. When the aircraft climbs the pressure reduces which is shown on the instrument as an increase in altitude (height).

The speed indicator is a tube pointing into the airflow and as the air goes down it a capsule fills up and expands...the faster the air is going down the tube the more it fills the capsule and the higher the indication of speed.

I used to fly a plane that had a small metal plate on a spring sticking into the airflow, as you went faster the airflow pushed the plate back against the spring, so you had to look out at the wing struts to see how fast you were flying.

The compass measures the same magnetic forces as a boy scout's compass except that it is made to a higher standard and the information is converted so that it can be shown on a dial. In fact all instruments on a modern airliner are electrically driven.

The most useful instrument is the attitude indicator. It shows if the aircraft is banking or is nose-up or nose-down. Modern altitude indicators give lots of other information as well, like speed, altitude and autopilot status. It's the instrument that's coloured blue and brown (sky and earth).

It shows attitude by measuring the phase shift of laser light going around prisms which are then electronically resolved into up and down and left and right movements.

Wow!

How much of the runway do the landing lights illuminate?

That's something I've never thought about. They show enough of what you want to see. I suppose the best description would be to say that they show more of the runway than car headlights show of the road in front of you. But they don't do that until you are over the runway. They don't show you where the runway is, the runway lights do that. They don't pick out the runway for you from a long way out if that's what you're asking.

How far away can you see an airport?

On a bright clear day and if you know what it looks like, you can identify one from about twelve to fifteen miles. Compared to a town or city they're quite small places.

Are some planes harder to fly than others?

Certainly, some are more complicated than others. But the skill to actually fly them is the same. Concorde pilots might tell you otherwise.

What are the tyre pressures on an aircraft?

The Boeings I flew were about 144 pounds per square inch.

How far can you see from the flight deck?

It depends upon the clearness of the air. Over Europe the air is not very clear but in Polar regions it's much cleaner and therefore clearer. On average you can see 80 to 120 miles on a good day. The tops of the Alps, for example, are visible a long way south of Genoa at a height of 30,000 feet or so. A Concorde pilot will tell you that he can see the curvature of the earth at its maximum height. What's more you don't have to ask him either…he'll just tell you anyway.

Are some airports safer than others?

No, but some have better instrument landing guidance systems or better lighting equipment or wider and longer runways. However, because commercial aircraft can only operate to those with a minimum standard, descriptions like better or worse, safe or unsafe don't actually come in to it.

What about hills and mountain ranges near airports?

That doesn't make any difference. A pilot isn't more careful because there are hills around, he's always careful. The hills or mountains make a difference with regard to what altitudes you descend to. You descend to the allowed altitudes like anywhere else; if the minimum altitude is 10,000 feet that's all you descend to. If it's 2,000 feet that's what you descend to. All these things have been calculated and the result is an approved approach procedure. A pilot doesn't have to work it out as he goes along.

Chapter Twelve

TECHNICALITIES

Will it help me to know something about the technical systems on the aircraft?

It might re-assure you to know that if something stops working that the aircraft won't just fall out of the sky.

There are four main systems on an aircraft:

➤ Engine
➤ Electrics
➤ Hydraulics
➤ Air

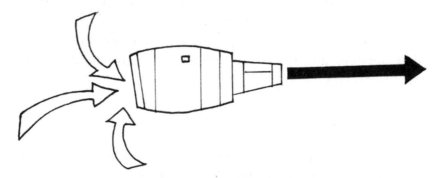

Cold air in...hot air out.

A jet engine works by sucking cold air into the front, heating it up in the middle and blowing the hot air out of the back. It pushes forward because the hot air goes out of the back quicker than the cold air goes in the front.

Does an aircraft move because it's being pushed along by the jet exhaust, not being driven along like the wheels on a car?

Yes. And when we taxi the aircraft we use very low power. In fact, you just have to release the brakes on some aircraft and it will start to move.

Shall I ask about electrics?

Please do: it's the subject I know least about.

Tell me about electrics on an aircraft.

You can either make electricity or you can store it. If you store it you use a battery and the batteries on an aircraft can give enough electrical power to last ninety minutes and keep all the important things going.

An aircraft makes its own electricity in the same way that a car does by using generators or alternators. Every engine has a generator so if one packs up, the other can meet all the needs of the aircraft. If they all pack up, the battery takes over automatically. Most of the electricity used on an aircraft is directed towards passenger comfort like in-flight entertainment, galley services and lights. The flight deck equipment uses very little electrical power.

Tell me gently about hydraulics because it sounds awful.

Hydraulics is the process of using liquid under pressure to exert a force that you couldn't manage on your own.

Like using a pressure hose to wash your car.

Like using a plunger to clear the sink.

If you have power steering on your car and you have owned a car without it then you'll know the benefits of power assistance.

Aircraft have hydraulic pumps on each engine.

The hydraulic systems power:

> ➤ The flying controls.
> ➤ The flaps.
> ➤ The raising and lowering of the wheels.
> ➤ The brakes.

Are there backup systems?

Yes. There are backups for everything. Hydraulic pumps can drive generators to give electricity. Generators can drive pumps to supply hydraulic power. Either of those systems can pump air. And air pumps can give electrical or hydraulic backup. So anything can do everything.

If you think of a water mill, the river flows by and turns the wheel, which turns an axle, which rotates the grinding wheels to squash the corn.

If you now think of a Mississippi paddle boat you can see the same principle. As the paddle wheel is driven round by the engine the boat moves through the water.

Combine the two and you've invented an hydraulic pump. If you fix the paddle steamer to the dockside and drive the paddle wheel round what will happen to the water? The water will be 'pumped' along. Stick a mill wheel into the flowing water and you've got an engine. And if you've got an engine you can pump fluids or air, or make electricity.

And finally the air system?

Each engine has an air pump which supplies air to the cabin so that we have enough oxygen to breathe. They also compress the air to make it warm.

Very warm air is circulated around the front of the wings, tail plane, fin and engine intakes to stop ice forming.

How do you navigate?

Navigation is done by the flight computer which is connected to the automatic pilot. There is a display unit with menus to select. Menus might ask you things like:

➤ Where are you now? (That's to set the equipment to the correct position before it starts to navigate on its own...but if you forget to update it...it'll remember where it was the last time it parked.)
➤ Where are you going?
➤ How much fuel do you have?
➤ Which route would you like to take from the following choices?
➤ Which runway are you taking off from and which one do you plan to land on?
➤ What height do you want to fly at?

Then it says 'leave the rest to me', the pilots then press 'engage' as soon as the aircraft is airborne and that's it.

What's the thing that you liked most about flying?

The view from my front seat window. The magnificence of the Alps. The wonder of ice-flows pouring from the land mass of Greenland into the sea. The stunning brilliance of the night sky. Watching the sun, moon and stars rise or set faster than on earth. The sun going down and then coming up again on a flight to the West Coast of America. Seeing the Pyramids. Flying along the Nile and seeing the effects of irrigation. Seeing the Eiffel Tower and the whole of Paris in one glance. Witnessing the cold landscape around Moscow. Doing an automatic landing, seeing nothing, and then hearing the passengers clapping. Being upside down in a bi-plane. Sending someone on their first solo flight.

But most of all getting myself, the crew, and the passengers to their destination as safely as possible.

What do you miss most?

Chatting to the passengers on the flight deck.

Chapter Fourteen

EMERGENCIES

What is an emergency?

An emergency situation would be any situation which if ignored would endanger the aircraft. However, there are circumstances, like an engine failure, that we have to treat as an emergency even though there is no immediate risk to the aircraft. That means we have to deal with it without delay.

An emergency is the highest category of malfunction on an aircraft but I'm certain that what you think is an emergency is not the same as my idea of one. Don't let uninformed newspaper stories influence you.

Have you had any?

No.

Do pilots practise them?

Yes. Every six months in the simulator we practise and are tested on all the emergency procedures. That would include engine failure during take-off, emergency descent and depressurisation and less critical things like flaps and wheels not working properly. And there would be routine problems like electrical and hydraulic failures.

Do pilots practise normal things?

Yes. One of the major leaps in simulator training has been the recognition that practising normal things is an effective way of learning.

A crew would be given an imaginary flight. They would be given an 'aircraft' that might have limitations imposed. The pilots, behaving as a normal crew would be expected to, find from their manuals the correct way to operate the 'flight' under the circumstances. During the 'flight' other problems are introduced, like a passenger being taken ill or a someone smoking in a toilet, and the crew have to make the sorts of decisions that they might have to take on a real flight. The entire 'flight' is recorded on videotape. After the 'flight' the crew are encouraged to discuss their decisions and behaviour with each other. This is done under the guidance and help of the training captain.

How hard is it to fly the aircraft if an engine stops during the take-off?

There are two procedures; one, if there's room to stop on the runway, and the other if you are 'going too fast' to stop. In the first case you close the throttles and put the brakes on, stop and call the fire services (just in case).

In the second where I deliberately used the words 'going too fast', you've nearly got enough speed to fly anyway so you just keep accelerating along the runway and take off normally. You have to keep the aircraft straight because it's trying to pull to one side. The aircraft is built so that the rudder is capable of doing that. Once the wheels are up, the pilots will then prepare to divert, continue to the destination, or land.

Is this the V1 speed…the point of no return?

Yes. Before the V1 speed we stop and after V1 we continue the take-off. The expression 'point of no return' is used in bad documentaries and Hollywood.

How hard is it to land if an engine has stopped?

It's as hard or as easy as pushing a supermarket trolley that won't steer straight and which keeps heading off to one side. Once you've worked out the angle to push it to get through the aisles and car park it's quite easy. We practise all the angles and things in the simulator, so we know what it's going to be like.

Next time you're in the supermarket imagine your trolley weighs a hundred tons and is travelling at 120 miles an hour and you can pretend you're flying on one engine.

I love supermarkets.

What do pilots have to do when there is a malfunction on board?

Problems that require immediate attention are the ones called Emergencies and the checklist procedures will ensure a safe outcome. Flying is not new and nearly all the emergencies have been identified now. Sticking to the book is the way to ensure success. Incidentally, pilots who do not comply with the laid-down procedures do not pass their competency checks and their licences become invalid.

What advice would you give to nervous passengers?

The reality is that flying is safe. My children never worried that I wasn't going to come home. Flying is just a job, and a safe one at that; it carries no extra insurance premiums. The people who fly aircraft are ordinary people who tend their gardens, have their hobbies, play CDs and watch the tele. They are not, and neither do they have to be, supermen or superwomen.

As I said at the start nothing ever happened to me or my crew that was beyond our ability to control. And the fact is, there was nothing ever likely to happen that would have been beyond us.

Finally and without wanting to make anyone more anxious than they are, here is the best advice you can get about flying and making it safer for you and your fellow passengers.

> Get on board and start taking notice of exits.
> Work out in your mind what you would do if you had to evacuate the aircraft.
> Read, read and re read the safety card.
> Rehearse your actions to evacuate.
> Don't be influenced by other people's stupidity when they don't bother to listen to the safety briefings.
> Do not hesitate to see your doctor about your anxieties if the sort of information offered in this book does not help you. She or he will be able to give you the proper guidance if your fears about flying are a phobia.

HELLO AGAIN, EVERYONE,

This is Keith the Captain, I hope that you have enjoyed this short flight with us today. Please have a safe onward journey and we look forward to seeing you again on one of our flights very soon.'

Bon voyage
Keith

And now will someone please write that book on boats so I can go on my retirement cruise?

Here are some questions I want to ask the captain.

- ➤ If we get a hole in the boat underwater how long will it be before I'm in a lifeboat?
- ➤ Does the lifeboat have an engine?
- ➤ Or a radio?
- ➤ Will I be with other passengers or will a member of the crew be allocated?
- ➤ How long has the captain been on duty and how well trained is the number two?
- ➤ How much fuel is on board?
- ➤ How powerful are the engines?
- ➤ How do you navigate into port?
- ➤ How do you steer sideways?
- ➤ Why don't you say upstairs and downstairs?
- ➤ Do you ever get seasick?

POSTSCRIPT

The world has changed since the 11th September 2001. Many lessons had not been learnt, many have now been and perhaps some remain to be learnt.

What we do know is that terrorists take advantage of breaches of security. However, what is not widely recognised is that such breaches have been committed not only by terrorists but by countless passengers who have unwittingly shown them the way through the system. To keep air travel as safe as possible maintain vigilance and stick to the security procedures. There is a great deal going on in the background concerning security measures which cannot be publicised.